NEGOTIATING
THE
IMPOSSIBLE

Deepak Malhotra is the Eli Goldston Professor of Business Administration at the Harvard Business School, where he teaches negotiation courses in a wide variety of programs. Deepak has won numerous awards for his teaching, including the HBS Faculty Award and the Charles M. Williams Award. In 2014, Deepak was chosen by *Poets & Quants* to be among their "40 under 40", a listing of the world's best business school professors under the age of 40.

Deepak's first book (with Max Bazerman), *Negotiation Genius,* was awarded the 2008 Outstanding Book Award by the International Institute for Conflict Prevention and Resolution. His second book, *I Moved Your Cheese,* was a *Wall Street Journal* bestseller and has sold translation rights in over twenty languages. Deepak's research on negotiation and dispute resolution has been published in top journals in the fields of management, psychology, conflict resolution and foreign policy.

Deepak's professional activities include training, consulting and advisory work in the areas of negotiation and deal making for firms across the globe. His advisory work in the area of policy focuses primarily on helping governments negotiate an end to armed conflicts. Deepak also teaches a course on negotiation, as a visiting professor, in the Blavatnik School of Government at the University of Oxford. Deepak's Twitter handle is @Prof_Malhotra

PRAISE FOR *NEGOTIATING THE IMPOSSIBLE*

"By using historically significant, seemingly intractable negotiations as examples, Malhotra provides practical lessons for the everyday negotiations in your life—including the three surprising 'levers' at your service when the use of force is not a viable option. This book is magic for any deal maker."

—Daniel H. Pink, author of *Drive* and *To Sell Is Human*

"If only we could lock the world's leaders in a room to read this book. Professor Malhotra's analysis of how negotiators can achieve the best possible outcomes for all sides is revelatory. It also starkly highlights what's missing in current negotiations—whether on refugees, on peace in Syria, or on Eurozone debt. This is a must-read for all practitioners of politics and public service."

—Ngaire Woods, Founding Dean of the Blavatnik School of Government at University of Oxford; Advisor to the IMF, UNDP and Commonwealth Heads of Government

"Packed with practical principles and illustrated with compelling examples, *Negotiating the Impossible* is one of the most useful and enjoyable negotiation books you will ever read!"

—William Ury, Co-Author of *Getting to Yes*

"Professor Malhotra is a rare academic with real expertise in the world of negotiation and diplomacy. He gets his hands dirty and has worked behind the scenes on some of the most difficult negotiations of our time. He sees what others don't see—and he has written it all down in *Negotiating the Impossible*."

—Jonathan Powell, former Chief-of-Staff to Tony Blair; chief British negotiator for Northern Ireland; Founder of Inter-Mediate; Author of *Talking to Terrorists*

"*Negotiating the Impossible* is a tour de force. Professor Malhotra is both a leading academic and an amazing storyteller; he has also been in the trenches and knows first-hand what it takes to tackle even the most difficult of situations. Whether you've done one deal or a hundred, this book will change how you negotiate. I will be giving it to everyone on my team."

—Vinod Khosla, venture capitalist, co-founder of Khosla Ventures

"Deepak Malhotra has done what few others could do: he draws upon the lessons of history to demonstrate that even the worst conflicts can be resolved. This book is especially significant because it gives both the inspiration and the tools you need to tackle extremely difficult negotiations."

—David Gergen, CNN Senior Political Analyst; Adviser to four U.S. Presidents; Co-director, Center for Public Leadership, Harvard Kennedy School

"If you want the best advice on how to negotiate when it looks like a deal can't be done, then *Negotiating the Impossible* is a must. It's filled with great strategies you can immediately put to use in your business and personal lives. It's also an extremely entertaining, thought-provoking book that you won't want to put down."

—Tyra Banks, CEO TYRA Beauty; Creator of America's Next Top Model

NEGOTIATING THE IMPOSSIBLE

HOW TO BREAK DEADLOCKS AND RESOLVE UGLY CONFLICTS WITHOUT MONEY OR MUSCLE

DEEPAK MALHOTRA
HARVARD BUSINESS SCHOOL

18 17
HARPER
BUSINESS

First published in paperback in 2016 by
Berrett-Koehler Publishers, Inc.

First published in India in 2016 by Collins Business
An Imprint of HarperCollins *Publishers* India

HarperCollins Publishers India, Cyber City, Building 10-A, Gurugram,
Haryana-122002, India
www.harpercollins.co.in

2 4 6 8 10 9 7 5 3

This edition published in India in 2018 by Harper Business

P-ISBN: 978-93-5264-017-1
E-ISBN: 978-93-5264-018-8

Interior Design and Book Production: Seventeenth Street Studios
Copyeditor: Mary Jean Haley
Indexer: Richard Evans
Proofreader: Elissa Rabellino

Printed and bound at
MicroPrints India, New Delhi

MIX
Paper
FSC FSC™ C218906

This product is made of FSC®-certified and other controlled material.

HarperCollins Publishers, Macken House, 39/40 Mayor Street
Upper, Dublin 1, D01 C9W8, Ireland

For Aisha, Aria, and Jai

Remember—every problem wants to be solved

CONTENTS

Preface ix

Introduction The Most Ancient Lesson in Peacemaking 1

PART I: THE POWER OF FRAMING

1 **The Power of Framing** 8
Negotiating in the NFL

2 **Leveraging the Power of Framing** 15
Stalemate over Royalty Rates

3 **The Logic of Appropriateness** 28
Negotiating in the Shadow of Cancer

4 **Strategic Ambiguity** 38
US–India Civil Nuclear Agreement

5 **The Limits of Framing** 45
Charting a Path to War in Iraq

6 **First-Mover Advantage** 51
The Unbroken Peace Treaty

PART II: THE POWER OF PROCESS

7 **The Power of Process** 60
Negotiating the US Constitution

8 **Leveraging the Power of Process** 68
Reneging on a $10 Million Handshake

9 **Preserve Forward Momentum** 80
Strikes and Lockouts in the NHL

10 **Stay at the Table** 89
Peacemaking from Vienna to Paris

11 **The Limits of Process** 98
Trying to End the Vietnam War

12 **Changing the Rules of Engagement** 109
Negotiating with Your Friends

PART III: THE POWER OF EMPATHY

13 **The Power of Empathy** 122
Negotiating the Cuban Missile Crisis

14 **Leveraging the Power of Empathy** 135
Deal Making with a Gun to Our Head

15 **Yielding** 149
Selling Modernity in Saudi Arabia

16 **Map Out the Negotiation Space** 156
Negotiating the Louisiana Purchase

17 **Partners, Not Opponents** 171
Caught in the Crossfire

18 **Compare the Maps** 180
Lessons in Cartography and Linguistics

19 **The Path Forward** 192

Notes 199

Index 205

Acknowledgments 210

PREFACE

IF YOU HAVE NEVER faced a difficult deadlock or ugly conflict in your life, consider yourself to be among the lucky few. But if you are like most people, you have encountered negotiations that seemed impossible, and you have struggled with some tough questions: How can you defuse a situation in which no one seems willing to back down? Is it possible to negotiate effectively when you have no money or power? If your attempts at negotiating in good faith are failing, what can you do? How might you deal with people who are acting aggressively or unethically, or who are simply unwilling to negotiate? How can you resolve protracted or escalating conflicts?

Over the years I have worked with tens of thousands of business owners, executives, and managers. I have consulted on hundreds of high-stakes negotiations, deadlocked deals, diplomatic stalemates, and protracted conflicts. And I have advised countless people who were dealing with challenging situations or difficult people in their work or daily lives. One question that people in all of these environments ask is how they can learn to negotiate more effectively when things seem hopeless. And while many books carry nuggets of insight on the topic, I have struggled to come up with an answer when asked to recommend a book that deals with especially challenging situations. I have not found a way to share my conviction that even the most difficult of negotiation problems have potential solutions.

That is why I wrote this book. It is an acknowledgment of the fact that while those of us who study negotiation have written a lot that is extremely useful, we may have ignored some of the most persistent and important questions. This book provides answers to those questions.

The lessons in this book are brought to life through stories of people who managed to negotiate the seemingly impossible *without* having had the money or muscle to solve the problem. Each chapter tells a different story—from history, business, diplomacy, sports, or popular culture—and each story yields a series of insights and principles. Whenever possible, I give additional examples of how these insights can be applied in other domains, whether you are negotiating with an employer or a spouse, a strategic partner or a child, a potential customer or a terrorist group. I have no doubt that you—the reader—will find additional, more personally relevant, applications.

I hope that the lessons in this book will help you resolve conflict, overcome deadlock, and achieve better outcomes in *all* of your negotiations—from the simple to the complex, and from the mundane to the seemingly impossible.

INTRODUCTION

The Most Ancient Lesson in Peacemaking

Among the oldest peace treaties in history is the Treaty of Kadesh, which was negotiated between the Egyptian and Hittite empires over three thousand years ago, in the middle of the 13th century BCE With neither party willing to continue incurring the costs of war, and with each side wary of looming conflict with its other neighbors, Pharaoh Ramesses II and King Hattusili III sought to negotiate an end to the conflict. Such attempts are difficult not only because the issues at stake may be contentious or complex, but because, often, neither side wants to make the first move. The side that comes asking for peace may look weak rather than wise or magnanimous, a signal that no leader can afford to send. And yet, a deal was reached. Despite having been drafted thousands of years ago, the treaty has many of the hallmarks of more recent agreements, including provisions proclaiming the end to conflict, the repatriation of refugees, an exchange of prisoners, and a mutual assistance pact if either side were to be attacked by others.[1]

One other characteristic makes this accord similar to what we often see today—in peace treaties, commercial agreements, and successful efforts at resolving conflicts ranging from international disputes to arguments between spouses. This feature is apparent in the Treaty of Kadesh only because it was recorded in two languages: hieroglyphics (the Egyptian translation) and Akkadian (the Hittite translation). A comparison of the translations reveals that the two versions are, as we ought to expect, very similar. But there is at least one important difference. The Egyptian translation states that it was the Hittites who came asking for peace terms. The Hittite version claims exactly the opposite.[2]

When it comes to deal making, diplomacy, and resolving disputes, it does not matter which culture you examine or what kind of negotiation you investigate. It does not matter why people were fighting or why they chose to settle their differences. Some things never change: *the need for all sides to declare victory* is at least as old as recorded history itself.

The Treaty of Kadesh also exposes a more fundamental insight about negotiation and peacemaking—one that lays the foundation for this book:

> Even seemingly impossible deadlocks and conflicts can be resolved if we shed the assumption that our only sources of leverage are money and muscle.

This is especially important to keep in mind when you are dealing with a situation that seems hopeless. When even your most generous offers are being rejected, when your well-intentioned attempts at addressing the issues are being thwarted, and when you have little power with which to impose a solution, you need a different approach and other sources of leverage. This book provides such an approach and reveals those sources of leverage.

THREE WAYS TO NEGOTIATE THE IMPOSSIBLE

Some negotiations are easy. Others are more difficult. And then there are situations that seem downright impossible. These are ones in which you have little power and limited options. These are times when conflict is escalating, deadlock is worsening, and no one is willing to back down. These are situations where people are behaving in ways that seem irrational—or worse, with clearly hostile intent. These are problems without precedent, where even vast experience offers limited guidance.

But these are also the cases that, when handled skillfully, will become the stuff of legend.

This book is about such negotiations: deadlocked deals and ugly disputes that seemed completely hopeless. Until, that is, someone found a way to beat the odds *without money or muscle.* What might we learn from these stories and from those who lived them?

As anyone who has dealt with deadlock or conflict will attest, some of the hardest situations to resolve are those where your attempts at negotiating in good faith have failed and where you don't have the resources or power to bargain effectively. The reason people lose hope and begin to see the situation as impossible is that they have already tried their best to address the substance of the dispute—they simply have no more money or muscle left. But what if there were other levers you could use?

In this book, we will focus on three crucial levers that negotiators often ignore, underestimate, or mismanage, especially when they are accustomed to thinking of power in terms of money and muscle:

- The Power of Framing
- The Power of Process
- The Power of Empathy

In my teaching and advisory work with thousands of business executives and company owners, I have heard countless tales of deal makers who were negotiating against the odds. In my work for governments and policy makers who are trying to negotiate with terrorists and armed insurgents, I have many times encountered the feeling of despair that comes from tackling the seemingly impossible. And, in my observations of even ordinary conflicts of everyday life, I have seen people struggle with how to manage hostile people, difficult situations, and thorny issues. In all of these places, people sometimes make a bad situation worse—or a difficult problem seem impossible—by pinning their hopes on money and muscle and failing to appreciate the power of framing, process, and empathy.

What insights might we share with people who are dealing with nasty conflicts in business, policy, diplomacy, or everyday life? What lessons might they learn from the most harrowing case of nuclear brinkmanship in world history? How might they emulate a young man of little clout or stature who managed to dominate one of the most important meetings of the last millennium? What might they take from the text of the most ancient peace treaty known to be in existence? What principles might they glean from comparing multibillion-dollar sports conflicts that were handled masterfully with those that ended in disaster? And what strategies might they borrow from a wide variety of high-stakes business disputes and deadlocks that were overcome without flexing muscle or throwing money at the problem?

The premise of the book is simple: there is much to be learned from situations in which people negotiated the "impossible." First, the stories themselves—from history, diplomacy, business, sports, and popular culture—are inherently interesting, and readers will learn about how people lived and fought and negotiated in times and places both near and distant from where we sit today. Second, the stories offer tangible lessons that can be applied by anyone who is dealing with his or her own conflict or deadlock, whether it is seemingly impossible or more ordinary. Throughout, I give examples of how the lessons could be applied in other domains—ranging from job offers, to business deals, to personal relationships, to negotiating with your children, to engaging with terrorists. Finally, if we were to strip this book of all its trappings, frameworks, and organizational structure, we would find that it is, at the core, a book about human beings trying their best to get along with each other in situations that are not always easy. My hope is that the book instills optimism and provides another lens through which the reader can begin to appreciate the sometimes puzzling, occasionally disappointing or even exasperating, yet often inspiring thing we call humanity.

RETHINKING "NEGOTIATION"

Before going any further, I will define *negotiation* as it is used in this book. In my experience, it is possible to think too narrowly about what negotiation is, what it entails, and when it is relevant—whereas I mean to use the word in its broadest possible sense. Too often, when people hear the word "negotiation," they equate it with haggling or debating, or imagine people in suits hammering out a deal. They think of negotiation as something we do once in a while—or worse, as a daunting or unpleasant task that should be avoided if possible. We would benefit from thinking differently.

Having advised on multibillion-dollar deals, I can say with confidence that negotiation is not about dollars and cents. Having advised on how heads of state might manage peace processes that are on the verge of collapse, I can tell you that negotiation is not about lives lost or lives saved. Having advised on job negotiations and family disputes and strategic partnerships and cease-fires, I can assure you that negotiation is not about career trajectory, or managing emotions, or finding synergies, or stopping bullets.

In short, negotiation is not about any one currency. Negotiation, regardless of the context or the issues involved, is fundamentally about *human interaction*. However simple or complex the issues, however well-intentioned or malicious the parties, however familiar or unprecedented the challenges, the question we are always trying to answer in negotiation is this: *How might we engage with other human beings in a way that leads to better understandings and agreements?* It does not matter whether the agreement is to be written down, as in a contract or treaty, or whether its enforcement is to be trusted to newly established goodwill, redesigned incentives, improved coordination, or merely the hope that accompanies a shaking of hands. It does not matter whether the understanding is between individuals or organizations, ethnic groups or countries. Negotiation is *always*, fundamentally, about human interaction. Sometimes these interactions are easy. Other times, they are tougher. And then, of course, there are the negotiations that interest us most in this book—the seemingly impossible ones.

Negotiation, then, is *the process by which two or more parties who perceive a difference in interests or perspective attempt to reach agreement*. The principles, strategies, and tactics that help us do so in extremely difficult situations are the focus of this book.

Deadlock and ugly conflicts

The book includes dozens of stories from many different contexts.[3] In selecting the examples, I have focused on the kinds of problems that people often admit to facing in their own lives: deadlocks and ugly conflicts. *Deadlock* is a situation where people are making incompatible demands and neither side is willing to back down. We will look at situations where the deadlock is so severe that it threatens the entire deal or relationship, but we will also tie the lessons back to less extreme situations. A conflict is any situation in which people have competing interests or divergent perspectives. *Ugly conflicts* are those in which people are facing formidable obstacles to achieving agreement—for example, mistrust, animosity, complexity, or a protracted history of hostility. We will see examples of each of these throughout the book as we extract lessons for managing conflicts of all kinds.

HOW THE BOOK IS ORGANIZED

The stories and lessons in this book are organized across three sections, each emphasizing and exploring one of the three levers: framing, process, and empathy. Which one of these levers will be the key to solving your problem—or, whether you will need to use multiple levers—will depend on the situation. Alone, each of these is extremely effective. Together, they provide a comprehensive approach to negotiating the impossible.

- *Part I* focuses on the **amazing potential of framing**. Effective negotiators know that *how* you articulate or structure your proposals can be as important as *what* you are proposing.
- *Part II* focuses on the **decisive role of process** in determining outcomes. Negotiating the process astutely can be more important than bargaining hard on the substance of the deal.
- *Part III* focuses on the **tremendous power of empathy**. A dispassionate and methodical approach to understanding the real interests and perspective of all relevant players can help to resolve even the ugliest of conflicts.[4]

Of course, not all problems of human interaction will be solved quickly or easily. Many of the worst conflicts require tremendous effort, strategic perseverance, and fortuitous timing. But there are also times when what is most needed is something a bit different: the ability to control the frame, to shape the process, and to unearth possibilities where others see none.

With that—I hope you enjoy the stories. I hope you find the lessons to be of value. And I hope the book encourages you to see every problem of human interaction as an opportunity for achieving greater understanding and better agreements.

Part I
THE POWER OF FRAMING

Yes, I have tricks in my pocket. I have things up my sleeve. But I am the opposite of a stage magician. He gives you illusion that has the appearance of truth. I give you truth in the pleasant disguise of illusion.

TOM WINGFIELD, IN
TENNESSEE WILLIAMS'S *THE GLASS MENAGERIE*

1

THE POWER OF FRAMING

Negotiating in the NFL

"YOU'VE GOT TO COME up with some new idea. You guys keep talking *past* each other instead of to each other."[1] These were the exasperated words of United States Magistrate Judge Arthur Boylan, who had been tasked with helping to end an escalating conflict between players and owners in the National Football League (NFL). It was May 2011, and team owners had already locked out the players. Much of the action was taking place in courtrooms, as each side tried to gain leverage through legal maneuverings. Ultimately, if a deal could not be struck, the coming season would be in jeopardy. This was not just a theoretical possibility: in 2005, a prolonged dispute between owners and players had decimated an entire season in the National Hockey League, eliminating more than $2 billion in projected revenue. The NFL had even more to lose, with approximately $10 billion standing in the balance.

With so much money at stake in professional sports, you can be assured that, once in a while, the action at the bargaining table will rival anything fans get to witness on the field. At issue in 2011 was the fate of the new collective bargaining agreement (CBA), a multiyear contract between owners and the players' union that governs the negotiation of individual contracts for all NFL players. The CBA also dictates, among other things, the revenue distribution between players and owners, the salary cap, minimum salaries, free agency rules, the terms of the annual draft, and working conditions. As in most CBA disputes in sports, one of the most salient and contentious issues in 2011 surrounded revenue sharing between owners and players. In other words, what percentage of the game's revenue should go to players and what percentage to owners? In this case, the owners were demanding a $2 billion off-the-top credit to support investments before any split of revenues would take place, after which the players would receive approximately 58% of what remained. Players wanted no off-the-top credit for owners, and a 50–50 split of *all revenues.*[2]

How do you resolve a dispute in which the demands of each party add up to more than is on the table—and neither side is willing to concede?

NEGOTIATING THE IMPOSSIBLE

The conflict escalated, and good faith bargaining gave way to legal maneuverings, heavy-handed tactics, and even appeals to the US Congress for intervention. Finally, there was a breakthrough. The resolution came when the parties agreed to a proposal (originating from the owners) that called for an entirely novel structure for revenue sharing. They decided that the way forward was to stop negotiating over "what percentage of all revenue" goes to each party. Instead, the parties would divide "all revenue" into three separate buckets that represented the different streams of NFL revenue. Then, they negotiated a different revenue sharing percentage for each bucket. The idea worked. The final agreement, signed August 4, 2011, states that players will receive:

- 55% of League Media revenue (e.g., revenue from TV rights)
- 45% of NFL Ventures / Postseason revenue (i.e., revenues from related businesses of the NFL)
- 40% of Local revenue (e.g., stadium revenue)

The solution, however, begs the question: What percentage of *all revenues* do the players receive from this deal? Running the numbers indicates that the three-buckets solution gives the players between 47% and 48% of all revenues in the first year of the contract. But wait! If that's the case, why go to all the trouble of creating three buckets with different percentages for each? Why not avoid the hassle of creating a new accounting system and simply agree to the players getting ~47.5% of all revenues?

There is an economically rational explanation for why three buckets may be a wiser solution than one big bucket. For example, consider what happens after the first year of the contract. If the players expect that League Media revenue will grow faster and hence represent a larger share of all revenues in the future, and the owners project that Local revenue will grow more rapidly, then the three-buckets approach is a value creating solution: it gives each side a higher percentage of the bucket it values most. The only problem with this economically rational explanation is that it has very little to do with why the two sides actually agreed to three buckets. We can be sure that the economically rational explanation falls short because when you read further down in the CBA, there is another provision that contains the following language:

> If, in any of the 2012–14 League Years, the Player Cost Amount... is greater than 48% of Projected "All Revenue" then the Player Cost Amount will be reduced to 48% of Projected "All Revenue." ... If, in any of these League Years, the Player Cost Amount is less than 47% of Projected "All Revenue", the Player Cost Amount shall be increased to 47% of Projected "All Revenue."

In other words, the two sides *are* agreeing to roughly 47.5% of all revenues going to players. If the percentage deviates in any meaningful way from 47.5% in any direction, it will be brought back to this relatively tight range.[3]

So we still have the same question: why go to the trouble of creating three buckets if the agreement is practically indistinguishable from what they could have achieved by agreeing to some specified percentage of all revenues for each year of the contract? To answer this, we need to first keep in mind that very few people actually look carefully at these kinds of contracts, and almost no media outlets comprehensively report or analyze the finer details of the deal. Second, while practically inconsequential, there is a small degree of movement possible in the revenue split in future years. Most importantly, the three-buckets approach is superior to the one-bucket approach in one essential respect: it allows each side to go back to its constituents and declare victory. It creates just enough room for league negotiators to report to the owners that they can keep a higher percentage of revenues where owner investments are greater (i.e., stadium-related revenues), and it lets Players Association negotiators announce that they get more than 50% of revenues whenever fans click on the television.

CONTROL THE FRAME

As the NFL example illustrates, even in difficult negotiations where the parties are deadlocked, stalemate might be overcome without the use of money or muscle.[4] Even though the argument was over money, the league did not have to keep throwing more dollars on the table to get the players to agree to the deal. Instead, what they did is a great illustration of the power of *framing*: objectively identical proposals can be made more or less attractive simply by how they are presented.

The "frame" of the negotiation is a *psychological lens*. It is a sense-making apparatus that influences how people perceive each other, the issues at hand, and the options that exist. There is almost no limit to the number and types of frames that can emerge in a negotiation. For example, negotiators may look at a deal through a financial or a strategic lens, see it from a short-term or a long-term perspective, or regard it as a friendly or hostile engagement. Likewise, diplomats may look at a problem from a political or a security point of view, as being a central or a peripheral concern, or in a historic or present-day context. Deal makers may evaluate a proposal relative to their initial aspirations for the deal, or how well it compares to what others have achieved, or how it will be judged by others.

There are no "right" or "wrong" frames, but which frame takes hold has important implications for how the parties behave and what they will ultimately be willing to accept. For example, sometimes a low-stakes issue that neither side really cares much about becomes infused with so much political or symbolic significance that neither side is willing or able to back down. In recent years, Democrats and Republicans in the United States Congress have been confronting this problem extensively: compromise on the slightest issue is considered by many partisans to be akin to wholesale betrayal, making it harder to reach agreements even where there is a lot at stake and plenty of bipartisan support on the substance of an issue.

Importantly, negotiators almost always have the power to influence the frame, and as we will see, *reframing* can be a powerful tool for overcoming barriers to deal making. Regardless of the objective stakes, much of what determines how people approach a problem depends on how they (or their constituents) *subjectively* make sense of it. Deal makers are unwilling to make concessions to perceived adversaries but are more amenable to doing so when they perceive the task as a collaborative problem-solving effort. Negotiators who frame a conflict as "winner takes all" will have a harder time than negotiators who believe it is possible for everyone to "win." Negotiators will be more or less willing to accept certain proposals when they adopt a short-term versus a long-term lens, or when the offer appears better versus worse than what they initially expected. As we discuss the power of framing throughout this section, we will pay particular attention to *how objectively identical proposals and options can be reframed to make them more attractive* to the other side. Paying attention not just to the substance of what is being negotiated, but also the lens through which parties are evaluating their options, can sometimes help break seemingly impossible deadlocks.

Control the frame of the negotiation. The frame that takes hold will shape how negotiators make decisions, evaluate options, and decide what is acceptable.

THE IMPORTANCE OF HELPING THE OTHER SIDE BACK DOWN

The problems that negotiators face in early stages of deal making can be quite different from the problems they face as talks progress. One critical difference relates to the reasons why someone stubbornly insists on making demands that you cannot possibly meet. When this happens early in a negotiation, it is usually a sign that you have failed to set appropriate expectations for what *is* possible. This can lead the other side to ask for the impossible—that is, to demand concessions that are true deal breakers for you. This is why it is a good idea to educate the other side *at the outset* about the limits of what you can offer and about the areas where you have more or less flexibility. Negotiators often fail to do this in the false belief that the other side is well-enough informed about the parameters of the negotiation, or because they are worried that discussing any limitations or constraints will raise doubts about their value as a partner. There may also be insufficient trust, making it harder for either side to believe that the other is genuinely so constrained, or that there is truly so little room for movement.

When people are *initially* deadlocked over incompatible positions, it usually means that their aspirations are unrealistic and there is simply not enough value on the table to meet them. If both sides want more than 50% of the pot, you have a serious problem, and the sooner you realize that it has nothing do with poor math skills, the better off you will be. This was undoubtedly the case in the NFL. The same problem frequently surfaces in diplomatic negotiations and business disputes.

But at some point in the process, perhaps after weeks of interaction, or months of trust building, or years of impasse, one or both parties may come to the conclusion that their earlier demands are not possible, and that major concessions will be needed to avoid a truly disastrous outcome. When that day comes, you may find that people are *still* unwilling to lower their demands. Now, you no longer have an education or trust problem to solve. The problem is how to get the other side to *admit* that they initially asked for more than was reasonable, and to back down and accept what is *actually* possible. The problem is all the worse when the other side will have to back down publicly, because they have committed to aggressive positions in front of others (e.g., their constituents or the media). In my experience, it is often relatively easier to get people to understand that they have overreached and that their demands are impossible to meet; it is a lot harder to get them to acknowledge this and change course. This was the problem that the NFL negotiators faced—and ultimately solved.

Convincing the other party that they will have to concede or withdraw from initial positions is not enough. You have to make it easier for them to back down.

NEGOTIATE STYLE AND STRUCTURE, NOT JUST THE SUBSTANCE

When the NFL negotiations were deadlocked, either side could have tried to make the deal more attractive to the other by reducing their own revenue demands. But this would have been a costly concession. As the solution they reached shows, you do not always have to throw money at the problem to move things along. Sometimes, wise concessions on style and structure can solve the problem more cheaply than costly concessions on substance. In this case, the three-buckets solution seems to have helped the parties accept a deal that did not seem palatable with a one-bucket structure, even though the objective value of the deal was almost identical. Negotiators who are mindful of style and structure are better positioned to overcome resistance, avoid impasse, and achieve better outcomes.

Wise concessions on style and structure can help solve a problem more cheaply than costly concessions on substance.

In the next chapter, we take a closer look at the various ways in which framing can help break deadlock without using money or muscle. In doing so, we derive more principles for resolving conflict of all kinds. We also devote particular attention to two factors that were at play in the NFL negotiations and that can make deadlocks especially difficult to break. First, there is the *audience problem*. The other side may be concerned not just with what they get from you, but also with how others will judge their acceptance of your offer. Second, there is the *zero-sum problem*. In a zero-sum situation the amount that one side gains must precisely equal what the other side loses.[5] When people are stuck negotiating over only one divisive issue, and there are no other interests involved, it becomes hard for them to make concessions without feeling they have lost and the other side has won. Let's see how these issues might be tackled.

2

LEVERAGING THE POWER OF FRAMING

Stalemate over Royalty Rates

WE WERE NEGOTIATING A large commercial agreement.[1] The company I was advising was an early-stage venture that had developed a potentially game-changing product in a multibillion-dollar industry. The folks on the other side of the table were hoping to license our product and help bring it to market. As a result, we had to negotiate a wide range of issues: licensing fee, royalty rate, exclusivity provisions, milestones, development commitments, and so on. We got stuck on royalty rate—that is, the percentage of sale price they would pay us for each product they sold.

There had been some early discussions in which the two sides had very informally agreed that a 5% royalty rate was reasonable. As time went on, it seemed that we had slightly different interpretations regarding how this percentage would be applied. Our view was that 5% was low, but would be acceptable as the rate they paid to us initially. As the product gained traction and was validated by the market, we felt the royalty rate should increase to a more appropriate, higher level. We understood that our technology was still in a development phase, that early sales momentum might be slow, and that their heavy investments in manufacturing warranted a concession from our side.

Their perspective was quite different. They argued that because of their investments, the royalty rate should initially be close to zero; after two to three years, the 5% rate would kick in; and after that, royalty rates should go *down*, not up. Why should they go down, we asked? "Because in our industry, we always see royalty rates go down over time, not up. That's just how it is," they replied. After some further probing they provided additional rationale: "If we are selling more of your product over time, you should be willing to accept a lower percentage."

Our initial hope was that we would be able to avoid confronting this issue head-on because the value of the overall deal was quite high, and with so much money to be made, this should not be a deal breaker for them. As the days passed with little progress, we realized that they really were stuck on the idea that "royalty rates are supposed to go down." Were they worried about the precedent this might set in their other deals? Was it something they had promised their board, and now they did not want to lose face? Were they simply trying to get better financial terms? Try as we might, we could not get the numbers to work with rates going down over time. And if we tried to accommodate their desire for lower rates in the first year or two, it further increased our need for higher rates later. What to do?

WITHOUT MONEY OR MUSCLE

There are times when two sides have incompatible positions and one has to yield. There are other times when each side compromises, meeting in the middle (for example, we could have agreed to a flat royalty rate over time). And then there are times when the laws of physics do not necessarily apply to negotiations: things can go up and down at the same time.

The breakthrough came when we noticed a flaw in how we were going about the discussion: we were stuck negotiating royalty rates in one dimension (*over time*), when our differing perspectives made clear that two dimensions were in play: the passage of *time* and the quantity of *sales*. Maybe we could leverage this to create a royalty schedule that went both up and down. If the other side needed to show rates going down over time, perhaps we could accommodate this and still safeguard our financial interests when the product sold more. With this in mind, we sent them a royalty table that no longer listed rates over time. Instead, we created a two-dimensional chart that listed rates as a function of time and quantity sold. It looked something like Table 1.[2]

TABLE 1

Quantity Sold	Year 1	Year 2	Year 3	Year 4	Year 5	...	Year 10
200,000	**9.5%**	**9.0%**	**8.5%**	**8.0%**	**7.5%**	...	**7.0%**
180,000	8	8	7	7	0		0
160,000	7	7	6	6	5		5
140,000	6	6	5	5	4		4
120,000	5	5	4	4	3		3
100,000	4	4	3	3	2		2
80,000	3	3	2	2	1		1
60,000	2	2	1	1	1		1
40,000	1	1	1	1	1		1
20,000	1	1	1	1	1		1
0	0	0	0	0	0	0	0

For each year, instead of one royalty rate we would have a range (with a minimum and maximum) based on quantity sold. Notably, the *maximum royalty rate* for each year would *decrease* over time (top row), which we hoped would meet their demand for diminishing royalty rates. At the same time, the *actual royalty rate* for each year could *increase* year after year if we sold more. Our expectations for how the royalty rates would actually materialize is shown in Table 2, with highlighted cells showing our internal projections.

TABLE 2

Quantity Sold	Year 1	Year 2	Year 3	Year 4	Year 5	. . .	Year 10
200,000	**9.5%**	**9.0%**	**8.5%**	**8.0%**	**7.5%**	**. . .**	**7.0%**
180,000	8	8	7	7	6		6
160,000	7	7	6	6	5		5
140,000	6	6	5	5	4		4
120,000	5	5	4	4	3		3
100,000	4	4	3	3	2		2
80,000	3	3	2	2	1		1
60,000	2	2	1	1	1		1
40,000	1	1	1	1	1		1
20,000	1	1	1	1	1		1
0	**0**	**0**	**0**	**0**	**0**		**0**

It worked. The other side argued over some of the numbers in the table, but this new proposal helped reframe our dialogue and avoid impasse. The two sides were no longer arguing over royalty trajectory or the rationale for whether it should go up or down, and in the weeks ahead, the issue went away completely. The final agreement contained a simplified version of the royalty table (with fewer columns and rows) that accounted for time and quantity. While perhaps not *substantively* different from what could have been accomplished by agreeing to royalty rates on one dimension, this *stylistic approach* helped our negotiating partner feel more comfortable with how the deal looked, and let us feel comfortable with the financial outcome.

PAY ATTENTION TO THE OPTICS OF THE DEAL

As this example illustrates, it's not just *what* you propose, but *how* you propose it. Too often, negotiators incorrectly assume that if you get the substance of the deal right—that is, your proposal is sufficiently valuable to the other side—then you do not have to worry about "how it looks," what we call the *optics of the deal*. But here, as in the NFL negotiations, the problem was not the value on the table, but the way the proposal was framed.

The role of optics is especially pronounced when there is an audience. The audience can be voters, the media, competitors, future negotiation partners, a boss, colleagues, or even friends and family. We are usually aware of our own audience, but we pay insufficient attention to theirs. In fact, their audience is just as important to consider as ours, especially if we are asking them to back down or make hefty concessions. To think of their audience as "their problem" ignores a central tenet of most difficult negotiations: there is no such thing as *their* problem; what seems to be their problem, if left unsolved, eventually becomes *your* problem. You may have already given them an offer that is superior to their alternatives, one that they "should" accept, but if you have not paid sufficient attention to the other factors that influence their decisions, you may find that even your generous offers are being rejected.

Pay attention to the optics of the deal. It's not just the substance of what you offer that matters, but how it looks to your negotiating partners and to their audience.

HELP THE OTHER SIDE SELL IT

In the 1991 book *Getting Past No*, William Ury uses a cogent phrase to highlight the importance of helping the other side with its audience. Ury tells us to "write their victory speech" for them. I always ask my students and clients to carefully consider not just how much value they are providing to the other side, but also how they and their audience will view an offer. *Think about how they can possibly say yes to what you are proposing and still declare victory.* If you cannot think of a way that they can construe the agreement as a "win," you may be in trouble.

This does not mean you should use stylistic or structural maneuvers to sell deals that are not in the best interest of either side's constituents. Later in this section we will tackle the possibility and problems of doing so, but for now, let us appreciate how everyone can benefit from effective framing. In the NFL example, reframing the proposal using three buckets helped create a narrative that the parties could use when they went home with what quite likely was the best deal they were going to get. Reframing helped avoid an impasse that could have resulted from negotiators being too concerned about their own image rather than what was best for their constituents. In our negotiations over royalty rates we were able to come up with a substantive proposal that worked for the other side, but they still needed help in framing the proposal so that nonsubstantive concerns would not derail it.

The same principle applies in less complex environments—for example, when you are negotiating a job offer. If the hiring manager is going to sweeten the deal or make an exception for you, he or she will need some way to justify it internally. I always remind my MBA students to help the other side with the arguments and narrative they need to explain why the concession they made was appropriate and necessary in this case.

Think about how the other side will sell the deal, and frame the proposal with their audience in mind.

MAKE IT SAFE FOR THE OTHER SIDE TO ASK FOR HELP

It is not always obvious whether the other side truly needs a substantive concession or merely has a problem with how your offer will look to their audiences. As you might also suspect, the other side is often unwilling to clarify which of these is the case. For them to admit that they don't absolutely *need* a substantive concession would be costly if we were already prepared to make one. Telling us that our proposal is, in fact, sufficiently valuable also undermines their argument for making further demands. Finally, revealing that they need help selling the deal could make them look weak, and may disrupt the deal process. These are all understandable concerns that might cause someone who is struggling with the optics to act as if the deal is simply not good enough.

If there is sufficient trust in the relationship, the other side is more likely to be candid about what is really standing in the way of the deal.

Even when there is little trust, a healthy degree of professional respect between the negotiators can help them signal to each other if they are stuck on the optics. Such signaling usually happens with a degree of plausible deniability; their signals will be ambiguous enough so that, if pushed, they can deny having such needs, but *you know and they know* that a message was sent.

It is important to remember that even these signals are hard to come by if you are seen as someone who always takes advantage of the slightest sign of weakness from the other side. To put it simply: *The safer you make it for the other party to tell you the truth, the more likely they are to do so.*[3] The best way to make it safe is to show them, through your actions, that you do not exploit every advantage you see, and that you appreciate the risks they are taking in being honest or transparent on important issues. In my experience, repeated negotiations or multiple deals over many months or years are not required for such reputations to be built; reputations for integrity and reliability are usually built in countless small ways throughout the process of even one deal. For example, you build trust by reciprocating when others have shared sensitive information or made a concession, by following through on your commitments, and by showing a willingness to be flexible when possible rather than fighting tooth and nail on every point.

Make it safe for the other side to ask for help on optics. Build a reputation for rewarding transparency and not exploiting their moments of weakness.

AVOID ONE-ISSUE NEGOTIATIONS

The royalty rate negotiation highlights a common problem in negotiations: getting stuck on one divisive issue. Counterintuitive as it may seem, negotiations are often easier when you have more than one thing to fight about. When there is only one issue on the table, and it is not easy to see how both sides can get what they want—or as much as they have promised to their audiences—you have a zero-sum problem in which at least one of you is going to feel or look like you lost. In these situations, it is useful to consider whether you can bring other issues to the table so that each side can walk away with something. When one of my children wants a toy that a sibling is playing with, I often advise him or her to bring along another toy to facilitate a potential trade. Arguing over who will get the one and only toy is not as likely to end well.

Alternatively, you might consider linking or combining what otherwise would have been two separate one-issue negotiations to create one easier negotiation rather than two more difficult ones. It is easier for my kids to agree on which TV show they will watch on Friday and Saturday if they discuss both days at the same time rather than having a separate conversation each day. What would be two separate arguments is replaced with one discussion in which each person gets something of value.

Sometimes, introducing even a relatively minor second issue is enough to dislodge the stalemate. The "win" you help to create for the other side need not always be as substantively valuable as what they give to you on the divisive issue. As noted, they may already be willing to live with you having your way on the divisive issue and are only looking for something—anything—around which to create a narrative that says "Both sides made concessions."

Avoid negotiating over a single divisive issue. Add issues or link separate one-issue negotiations.

NEGOTIATE MULTIPLE ISSUES SIMULTANEOUSLY

Even if there are multiple issues in the negotiation, if I have to concede on the issue we are discussing now in the hope that you will concede on the issue to be discussed later, I may be unwilling to take that risk. To address such concerns, it is usually wise to *negotiate multiple issues simultaneously*. In other words, instead of trying to reach agreement one issue at a time, create the habit of making "package" offers and counteroffers. For example, "Here is what we can do on Issue A, here is where we need to be on Issue B, and here is what we can accommodate on Issue C." This serves two purposes. First, as mentioned, it eliminates the risk that a concession made now will not be reciprocated later—you can make your concession contingent on theirs. Second, with multiple issues in the mix during the same discussion, it becomes easier for negotiators to make wise trades across issues—you can fight for what you care about more in exchange for giving up what the other side values more. In contrast, when you negotiate one issue at a time, people will often fight equally hard for whatever happens to be on the table at that time, making it difficult to find out what each side really cares about most.

For example, if I'm negotiating a complex business deal and someone tries to negotiate on one issue in isolation (e.g., price), I will usually shift the conversation to include other issues. There are many ways to do this. I can simply say that my position on price depends on where we are on other terms, so we need to discuss those issues as well before we try to finalize the price. I can make a "package" offer that includes terms other than price and clarify that my stated price assumes the following terms. I can present multiple offers, each with a different price and different terms, so the other side can better understand how the issues are related and how much flexibility I have. Any of these tactics can help us avoid getting bogged down on one divisive issue.

Negotiate multiple issues simultaneously to help identify wise trades and to reduce the risk that concessions will not be reciprocated.

DIFFUSE THE SPOTLIGHT

With multiple issues on the table, it is easier to construct an agreement that allows each side to show some wins. Unfortunately, even with multiple issues, one issue sometimes becomes the most prominent, and everyone starts using it as the sole measure of who wins and who loses. This was precisely the problem in the NFL negotiations; even if one side received monumental concessions on other issues, most observers would still use the revenue-split issue as the only barometer of success.

We also see this when political parties are negotiating over legislation. The reason it happens can vary. Sometimes the media or other audiences have limited information or expertise to judge anything other than one prominent issue. Other times, regrettably, the negotiators themselves inflate the importance of a single issue in their rhetoric. Politicians might do this to drum up enthusiasm among supporters, or deal makers may inadvertently do so as they try to efficiently articulate their positions. In some cases the problem arises even when there is no audience; one issue becomes prominent because one or both sides have overstated its importance to justify an aggressive opening position.

Don't let any single issue become too prominent. Educate your audiences about how to measure success, and limit the amount of attention given to any one issue.

SPLIT ONE ISSUE INTO TWO

Of course, there are situations where one issue *is* objectively the most important. And there are situations where, try as you may, no other issues are relevant (or possible to include) in the discussion. Even in these cases there is another strategy for avoiding a win/lose outcome: split the one issue into two or more. This is what the NFL negotiators did by splitting one revenue number into three separate revenue "buckets." We did something similar in the commercial agreement discussion: splitting "royalty rate per year" into "royalty scale per year" *and* "royalty based on quantity." And going back to the example of children and their toys: if there is only one toy, you might "split one issue into two" by discussing who gets the toy now and who gets it later. (Note: it is usually not as effective to actually break the toy into two pieces, although there are exceptions to this.)

If there is only one issue, try to split it into two or more separate issues.

UNMASK THE UNDERLYING INTERESTS

What seems like one contentious issue is sometimes composed of multiple hidden interests that *are* reconcilable. In such situations, you may be able to overcome stalemate by unmasking the underlying interests. For example, consider an employee who is haggling over an increase in salary with an employer who is clearly unwilling to agree to the raise. The reason may be that the employer does not think the employee deserves such a large increase in pay. If so, one option would be for the two of them to "meet in the middle" and find an amount they can both live with. If they can't find such a number, they may have to go their separate ways. But what if the employer thinks the employee's demand *is* fair, and the only reason she is saying no to the initial ask is that her budget is limited for this year? In that case, instead of meeting in the middle, it may be wise to split the issue into "salary this year" and "salary next year." This way, the employer can delay a hit to the budget, and the employee gets a much higher salary starting the following year.

In other words, it may be possible for both sides to meet their underlying interests (getting a higher raise, staying within budget), but this will only happen if they stop arguing about "what they want," and start discussing their motivations for "why they want it." This is referred to as shifting from *positions* (what people want) to *interests* (why they want it). Even when you have opposing positions on an issue, you might have compatible interests. The sooner you shift from arguing over positions to exploring underlying interests, the more quickly you will ascertain whether the needs of both sides can be reconciled.

Incompatible positions might be hiding reconcilable underlying interests. Understanding why the other side wants something can lead to better outcomes than continuing to argue over competing demands or trying to meet in the middle.

FIRM ON SUBSTANCE, FLEXIBLE ON STRUCTURE

Effective negotiators are assertive where needed and flexible when possible. After you have evaluated what each side brings to the table, and after you have considered what would be fair to demand, be as firm as necessary on *what* you deserve. But your assertiveness on substance should not spill over into stubbornness regarding *how* your demands are met. As the NFL and royalty rate examples demonstrate, the less demanding you are on the precise structure of the agreement, the more likely you are to find a deal that works for everyone. This flexibility gives the other side more options and makes it more likely that they can find *some* way to meet your needs. In my experience, a useful message to send to the other party, in both words and deeds throughout the negotiation, is this: *I know where I need to get; I'm flexible on how we get there.* To put it another way: the more currencies you allow them to pay you in, the more likely you are to get paid.

Be as firm as needed on substance; be as flexible as possible on style and structure.

GETTING UNSTUCK IS A WORTHY ENOUGH SHORT-TERM GOAL

You may have noticed that our offer to negotiate royalty rates in two dimensions instead of one did not immediately solve the problem. Instead, the other side pushed back on elements of the structure and found faults with this proposal, not the least of which was the fact that the numbers were too high for them. But what the proposal *did* accomplish was getting us unstuck on the divisive issue. We were now discussing matters that were substantive and ultimately reconcilable. This is an important point: crafting proposals that are sensitive to the other side's audience needs and which help to maneuver around divisive issues will not necessarily resolve the entire conflict or seal the entire deal. These proposals will, however, reduce the amount of time spent in deadlock and make it more likely that a mutually acceptable agreement can be found.

A wisely framed proposal need not resolve the entire dispute. Sometimes just getting unstuck is the key to paving the path towards eventual agreement.

In the examples considered so far, deadlock was caused by the two sides having opposing objectives, which led them to make demands that seemed irreconcilable. But it is possible to have deadlock even when the interests of everyone in the room are aligned and everyone is working towards the same objective. People might still disagree about the best way to *achieve* that objective. This might happen because there is insufficient trust, or because people are not effectively articulating the merits of their proposals, or because everyone has strong, and different, prior beliefs about the right path to take. We will see a number of these factors at play in the next chapter, in a domain of human interaction that is quite different from the situations we have considered so far. Let's see how framing tactics can help overcome psychological resistance to ideas that are new, foreign, or different from a person's existing beliefs or expectations.

3

THE LOGIC OF APPROPRIATENESS

Negotiating in the Shadow of Cancer

YOU MAY HAVE THE best, most innovative proposal, but how do you present it to someone who insists on doing things the way they've always been done? You may have the person's best interest in mind, but how can you negotiate in the face of severe resistance to change? You may be right, but how do you make your case when the other side is emotionally attached to an alternative course of action?

Consider the case of patients who are diagnosed with low-risk prostate cancer.[1] Most prostate cancer cases in the United States are detected using a screening test called the prostate-specific antigen test (PSA).[2] There is considerable evidence that many PSA-detected cancers are overdiagnosed—that is, the patient would have lived out the natural course of his life without ever knowing he had prostate cancer if not for having taken the PSA test.[3] At Memorial Sloan Kettering Cancer Center (MSKCC) in New York, one of the preeminent institutions in cancer research and treatment, "active surveillance" is generally recommended for men with low-risk prostate cancer—and is preferred over treatments such as surgery and radiotherapy that can cause side effects, including incontinence and erectile dysfunction. This recommendation is consistent with the National Comprehensive Cancer Network guidelines and the American Urology Association guidelines.

In active surveillance (AS), patients are carefully monitored with PSA tests, repeat biopsies, and physical examinations; if there is a sign that the disease has progressed to a higher risk category, patients are recommended for treatment (e.g., surgery or radiation therapy). An AS program typically includes lab tests and exams every six months, and a repeat biopsy every two years, to detect any disease progression.

When Dr. Behfar Ehdaie, MD, MPH, began practicing surgery at MSKCC, he found that only about 60% of the patients for whom he had recommended AS complied; all others opted for surgery or radiation and were unwilling to accept active surveillance as recommended. Other doctors at MSKCC had similar rates of compliance when they recommended AS. Moreover—and understandably—even the discussions a doctor would have with patients who *agreed* to AS were lengthy and difficult. Why were so many patients unwilling to accept an expert's recommendation, even though the doctor would arguably have made more money by proposing surgery, and even though surgery and radiation have significant quality-of-life detriments? What could be done differently to achieve better patient outcomes?

WITHOUT MONEY OR MUSCLE

Dr. Ehdaie and his collaborator, Dr. Andrew Vickers, started experimenting with ways to improve how AS is discussed with patients. When Dr. Ehdaie reached out to me, he wanted to work together on refining his approach to discussing AS, and more generally, on helping other doctors improve their communication with patients. Note that his goal was *not* to get other doctors to prescribe AS or any other remedy—that is a choice for each doctor to make—but to help physicians be more effective in making whatever recommendation they considered appropriate.[4]

The core problem, it seemed, was that patients were being asked to consider an option that was different from what they had initially assumed they would or should choose. How to overcome this resistance? How could we help patients more carefully consider doing what is in their own best interest? Building on ideas Dr. Ehdaie had already started to implement, we worked together to refine the approach based on existing research in psychology and on my experience helping organizations articulate their value proposition to customers and stakeholders. The results have been quite striking. Since changing the conversation in the room, according to data collected over three months, adoption of AS by Dr. Ehdaie's patients has increased from about 60% to 95%. And what did it cost him to implement the change? *Less than nothing.* First, the new approach did not require any costly changes to policy, administrative structure, or interactions between doctors, hospitals, and insurance companies. In addition, his average counseling time for low-risk patients actually *decreased* to around 35 minutes compared to over 60 minutes prior to implementing the new approach. The conversations were not only more effective, but also more efficient.

Here I share some of the principles that Dr. Ehdaie now applies in his communication with patients to keep the conversation from getting derailed.[5] In particular, I focus on how the options are reframed to overcome resistance to change. When blended together, these principles are like a "recipe" for dealing with resistance to ideas, not just in this setting, but in all kinds of negotiations.

THE LOGIC OF APPROPRIATENESS

How do people make decisions? How do they decide whether to say "Yes" or "No," to choose "A" or "B," or to act rather than do nothing? We are all familiar with one way people choose: cost-benefit analysis. The basic idea is that people weigh the costs and benefits of all options and pick the one that seems to be best overall, perhaps with some adjustment based on risk preferences. But is that really how people behave all, or even most, of the time? Social scientists James March and Johan Olsen have an alternative model for decision making, which they refer to as the *logic of appropriateness.*[6] They suggest that, rather than engaging in a potentially complex or time-consuming cost-benefit analysis, people often make decisions by asking themselves a simple question: "What does a person like me do in a situation like this?"[7] Whatever answer comes to mind when this question is posed has a significant influence on how people choose to behave.

If we take the *logic of appropriateness* seriously, it means that we should be mindful of whether people will perceive our offer or preferred option as "appropriate," and also of how we might boost the appropriateness of the proposals we make. A large body of work in psychology (and more recently, in behavioral economics) looks at the topic of persuasion and how choices can be framed to make them more compelling. In my work with Dr. Ehdaie, we introduced three of these ideas to boost the appropriateness of AS. I've added a fourth here that is not as directly relevant to negotiation with patients but is very important across many negotiation contexts. These principles, based on my experience, are among the most powerful and broadly applicable means of boosting the appropriateness—and hence the attractiveness—of an idea or proposal.[8]

The logic of appropriateness tells us that many of the choices people make are based on how they answer one simple question: What does a person like me do in a situation like this?

1: LEVERAGE SOCIAL PROOF

The principle of "social proof," as articulated by social psychologist Robert Cialdini, says that when people are unsure about which way to go, or what to choose, they look to the behavior of others, actual or implied.[9] According to the logic of appropriateness, if we think most others are actually doing something, it must be appropriate. This is because when people look at the world, they think *the world is supposed to make sense.* And so when they see other people choosing a certain course of action, they say to themselves, "There must be a reason," and take it as a signal that it is the correct or normal or acceptable behavior. Not surprisingly, then, the most direct way to boost the appropriateness of an option is to demonstrate or signal that others are also choosing it. Dr. Ehdaie describes how, prior to revising his approach, the principle of social proof was actually working against him. His earlier efforts to highlight what makes MSKCC unique were turning patients off to the idea of AS. He changed his language to take the power of social proof into account:

> Before, I would tell patients something like "most men in the United States do not choose active surveillance because they are worried that cancer would spread or physicians feel uncomfortable not recommending surgery or radiation. However, at MSKCC, we are committed to maintaining your quality of life *and* treating your cancer; therefore we recommend surgery or radiation only to men who we know will

benefit." Unfortunately, all they heard was "most men do not choose active surveillance," and they stopped paying attention after that. Given the success I have had with my new approach, I am now able to articulate a very compelling argument. I emphasize that the vast majority of men like them choose active surveillance in my clinic and that I follow more than 300 men per year.[10]

Leverage social proof to boost the appropriateness of your proposal.

The promise and peril of uniqueness

In business negotiations, the same principle is prevalent. For example, most people know that "being innovative" can be a source of attraction and leverage. But as the patients' example shows, in our rush to portray our solution as unique, path-breaking, and better than the competition, we sometimes inadvertently shoot ourselves in the foot. A salesperson, for example, who is trying to convince the customer that she will have the advantage of being among the first adopters of a new technology or solution may find that the strength of this pitch is eroded (or wiped out completely) by the fact that the other side is implicitly hearing "Other people like me don't do this," and thinking "What do they know that I don't?" or "There must be no urgency to do this." A salesperson in this situation may need to counterbalance the "uniqueness" argument with other information that can allay such concerns.

Framing an option as unique might make it more intriguing but less attractive.

2: SET THE DEFAULT OPTION

Default options are another marker of appropriateness. When something is the presumptive or preset choice in a setting, it leads people to conclude "It must be the default for a reason"— that is, it must be what most others do, or it is normal or acceptable. Research has shown that people are strongly influenced by default options. Even when they are completely free to choose whatever they want, it seems that shifting away from the default (i.e., the status quo) is psychologically taxing. Whether people are choosing between different strategies or different product offerings, you can boost an option's appropriateness by making it the default. To be precise, the principle does not say that the default option is always the *most* attractive option, but that an option's attractiveness is *enhanced* when it becomes the default. With prostate cancer, for example, when the patient enters the room, surgery is often the default option in his mind. The conversation will be much easier if you can shift the default to AS at the very beginning of the conversation. To allow surgery to persist as the default and to later try and muster reasons for moving away from it may be an uphill battle. Here is how Dr. Ehdaie describes his implementation of this principle:

> When it comes to discussing options, I now introduce active surveillance as the default choice and focus on it first. Specifically, I reassure patients that they have low-risk prostate cancer as compared to other men with high risk disease and say, "In men like you with low-risk prostate cancer, we recommend active surveillance, and for other men with higher-risk prostate cancer, we recommend surgery or radiation. Today, I want to focus on active surveillance, but I can also answer questions about surgery or radiation. [11]

Present your proposal as the default option to boost its appropriateness.

Start with your draft of the agreement or process

When you are negotiating a contract, who sets the default? Where does it reside? Usually, it is in the hands of whichever party drafts the initial version of the contract or whichever party's *boilerplate* (i.e., standard contract) you are using. There is a clear advantage to being the party who presents the initial draft or whose standard contract will be used as the template for the deal. In my experience, many items that reside in boilerplates—even some important provisions that have a substantive impact on the value of the deal—often go unchallenged or, because they are included in the standard contract, are not haggled over as aggressively as they would be had they only been proposed orally by the other side. There is a natural tendency to think, "If it is in their boilerplate, it must be there for a reason. Perhaps this is normal. This is probably something most people are willing to accept."

Relatedly, in the academic literature on negotiation, among the most widely studied tactics is what is known as "anchoring," which typically refers to the idea that the first offer from either side will powerfully frame the negotiation and shape the other side's perception about what is possible and acceptable in the deal. As a result, the final outcomes of a negotiation (e.g., the price of an asset) are often correlated with first offers.[12]

Default proposals or expectations are also relevant to how a negotiation *process* should be structured—for example, timetables for completing the deal, who will be involved in the negotiation, which side will make the opening offer, what will be on the agenda, and so on. In most cases, there are preexisting expectations or standards for such choices based on precedent. It behooves negotiators to evaluate existing defaults, and to try to shift them if necessary. As with other factors that influence framing, the longer a default persists, the harder it is to change. If you can shift the default before the other party enters the room, all the better. If you cannot, move quickly to shift perceptions regarding the default at the outset of negotiations. For this reason, Dr. Ehdaie now tries to shift the default from "surgery" to "active surveillance" as early as possible in the conversation.

The party that drafts the initial version of the agreement or process gains leverage.

3: SHIFT THE REFERENCE POINT

Is $10,000 a lot of money? It can be a hard question to answer definitively because it depends on what you are comparing it to or contemplating. If you are thinking about buying a watch, it is a lot of money and the amount will be very salient; if you're buying a house or discussing the national debt, then it is not particularly attention worthy. The point is that people do not react to or evaluate data and options in a vacuum. Someone who is evaluating an offer, the suitability of a timetable, or the level of success achieved on a performance metric always has some reference point in mind. If it is the "wrong" reference point, even the best data or the most meritorious argument will be evaluated as weak. Before presenting your information, then, it is wise to set an appropriate reference point. As Dr. Ehdaie explains:

> In the past, when I would explain that active surveillance entails six-month follow-ups, the patients and their families would immediately get alarmed that this did not seem like "close" monitoring and that the cancer might spread in the six months between appointments. The discussion would shift to a very defensive posture, where I would be arguing that maybe it *could* spread in six months but this was very, very improbable. Now, before I discuss the follow-plan at the end of the discussion, I say, "PSA screening has enabled us to detect prostate cancer four to six years before it would have been diagnosed clinically. Furthermore, in men with prostate cancer who were never treated, changes in their prostate cancer, or progression, occurred usually after 10 years. Therefore, it would even be safe to see you again in five years; however, we will be aggressive about how closely we monitor you and plan to see you back every six months." Previously, six months seemed like an eternity to patients. With the proper frame of reference, which is derived from the natural history of prostate cancer progression, six months now is understood to be a short time between follow-ups.[13]

Whether you are negotiating a business deal, in armed conflict, or in the doctor's office, the reference point that is in the mind of the recipient can determine whether your proposal will be perceived as balanced or one-sided, generous or unfair, comforting or anxiety-provoking. It is important for negotiators to ensure that the other party is evaluating the substance of what is being offered within an appropriate context. There is always a context in which the proposal will be evaluated—there is *always* a reference point. As with defaults, it is worth asking whether a preexisting reference point is appropriate or useful, or whether it needs to be reset.

Establish a proper reference point. Even generous proposals can be evaluated negatively if the other side's reference point is not set appropriately.

4: DON'T APOLOGIZE FOR YOUR OFFER

It does a doctor little good if she gives the best advice possible, but then undermines it by seeming apologetic for having proposed something the patient does not like. The same is true in negotiations of all types. For example, I've worked with a number of companies that have innovative products and services, and in many cases, this puts their price point as much as ten times higher than that of their competitors. Inevitably, when the salesperson first mentions a high price, the customer's reaction is some mix of surprise, disappointment, and annoyance. "No one pays that much for this type of thing." At this point, the worst mistake a salesperson can make is to appear apologetic for the high price point. Yet salespeople do this often, perhaps because they are unprepared for the pushback and are put on the defensive, or perhaps because they are trying to appear sympathetic. There are many words and deeds that convey an apology: responding with, "I know it's a high price, but . . ."; too quickly expressing a willingness to negotiate price if necessary; getting derailed from the initial pitch surrounding the value proposition; getting into a discussion about what others are charging; or simply losing confidence in tone. So what should a salesperson do instead?

In sales and in negotiations of all sorts, if you've crafted your proposal carefully and think it is appropriate, *don't apologize for it.* The moment you seem apologetic, you give the other side the license to start haggling. This does not mean you should be unwilling to negotiate price. Nor does it mean you shouldn't *explain* your price. But when you apologize for your offer, you are creating a frame that says your proposal is inappropriate and that *even you* do not think it is a reasonable starting point. If you are bringing more to the table than competing offers, you want to shift the frame to a discussion of value. For example, if the customer complains about the price being too high, the salesperson might say, "I think what you're wondering is, how is it that despite having this price we have so many people lining up to buy our product? What kind of value are we delivering that allows us to win so many deals over our competitors? I'm happy to have that conversation. At the end of the day, we both know that nobody will ever pay more than something is worth. So let's discuss the value proposition..."

Always justify your offer, but don't apologize for it.

As a final point regarding the tools for boosting appropriateness, it is worth considering the ethics of framing. Dr. Ehdaie's objectives were clearly benevolent. In other contexts, however, we must consider when framing is appropriate and when it might be unscrupulous. Any time you are helping to shape the choice someone else makes, it is essential to evaluate not only your own *intentions* but also *all of the consequences* that will follow. In the examples so far, we have tried to focus on negotiators who have used framing tactics to help *all* of the parties overcome deadlock and achieve value-creating outcomes.

This does not mean that these principles cannot be applied in nefarious ways—either due to ill intentions or because of the failure to consider how others will be affected. (We will consider such a situation later in this section.) The good news is that it is not so easy to persuade people to choose a course of action that is bad for them simply via framing. In the vast majority of cases, and as evidenced throughout the examples we have considered, framing works best when the party you are targeting is willing, and perhaps even hoping, to move in the direction you are steering them—if only you can make it easy for them.

On the other hand, it is not always the case that the other side is willing to accommodate your substantive demands as long as you can accommodate them on style and structure. In some cases, unfortunately, both sides have strongly held views or severe constraints, and neither side can afford to accept the other's position. How might the power of framing help then? We consider this in the next chapter.

4

STRATEGIC AMBIGUITY

US–India Civil Nuclear Agreement

IN 1968, THE "TREATY on the Non-Proliferation of Nuclear Weapons," more commonly known as the *Non-Proliferation Treaty* (NPT), was negotiated into existence. The NPT was designed to restrict the number of countries that would have access to nuclear weapons to the five countries that had them at the time: the United States, the United Kingdom, the Soviet Union, France, and China. Not coincidentally, these were also the five permanent members of the United Nations Security Council. The long-term vision of the NPT was that signatories would commit (a) not to engage in proliferation activities, (b) to eventual disarmament among those who currently had nuclear weapons, (c) to supporting the peaceful use of nuclear technology for all signatories, and (d) to submit to inspections and safeguards by the International Atomic Energy Agency (IAEA) to ensure safety and compliance.

By the turn of the century, 190 countries had signed the NPT, with the only holdouts at the time being North Korea, Israel, Pakistan, and India.[1] Those who refused to sign argued, as did many signatories, that given insufficient commitment to disarmament by the *nuclear haves*, the treaty was simply suppressing the sovereign and strategic rights of nuclear *have-nots*. In the years since the NPT went into effect, each of these four nonsignatories had, with varying degrees of success, developed its own nuclear weapons.

In July 2005, the United States and India set in motion what would become a three-year marathon of interrelated negotiations aimed at completing a "civilian nuclear agreement" between the two countries.[2] The premise was relatively straightforward: India would agree to separate its military and civilian nuclear facilities and place the latter under IAEA safeguards in exchange for full civil (i.e., nonmilitary) nuclear cooperation (e.g., commerce) by the United States and the then-45-nation Nuclear Suppliers Group (NSG). India's status as a nonsignatory to the NPT, however, made the negotiations difficult—some would have said inconceivable. To allow India to engage in civil nuclear commerce would, in the view of many, undermine American commitment to the NPT. If nonsignatories would be treated as well as signatories, what incentive would there be for anyone to sign? In contrast, the Bush administration and others among the NSG believed that despite being a nonsignatory of the NPT, and despite having developed its own weapons, India had not engaged in proliferation activities. Allowing it to participate in civilian nuclear commerce in exchange for some degree of IAEA inspections and safeguards would only promote continued responsible behavior and greater safety.

Reaching such an agreement was meant to be difficult. Negotiations would need to be coordinated and sequenced at many levels, across the globe. First, the United States would have to pass domestic legislation allowing it to engage with a nonsignatory of the NPT (accomplished via the *Hyde Act* in 2006). Then, the United States and India would have to negotiate a bilateral agreement (referred to as a *123 Agreement*). Meanwhile, the IAEA would have to approve an agreement with India to place Indian civil nuclear facilities under IAEA safeguards, and the NSG would have to grant India an unprecedented waiver to allow it to have access to nuclear technology and fuel. Finally, the agreement between US and Indian diplomats would have to be approved by the US Congress and supported by India's Parliament.

One of the more vexing problems that arose during these negotiations pertained to the consequences that would follow if India tested another nuclear weapon. In 1998, India had, to broad international condemnation, conducted five nuclear tests, resulting not only in sanctions by the United States and others, but also in retaliatory nuclear tests (for the first time) by Pakistan, a mere two weeks later. A year later, in 1999, due to Pakistani military incursions through the "Line of Control" separating India and Pakistan in Kashmir, the two had waged history's first and only conventional war between known nuclear powers. With this terrifying backdrop in place, it is no surprise that support for the civil nuclear agreement among US lawmakers and many NSG nations was contingent upon guarantees that India would not test another nuclear weapon.[3]

Meanwhile, support in India was contingent upon exactly the *opposite.* There seemed no possibility that India's Parliament would approve a deal if the agreement limited their perceived sovereign right to test nuclear weapons if and when they felt it was necessary. Indeed, this was the very reason India had not signed the NPT in the first place: a civil nuclear agreement that imposed NPT-type restrictions was entirely unacceptable. India had announced a voluntary moratorium on testing but was unwilling to make the moratorium binding.

How do you negotiate an agreement when the exact same issue is a deal breaker for both sides? How can you reconcile the interests of both parties when the minimum requirements of one (based on the logic of *international security*) are entirely unacceptable to the other (based on the logic of *national sovereignty*)?

WITHOUT MONEY OR MUSCLE

In 2007, the United States and India negotiated their bilateral agreement; in 2008, the government of Prime Minister Singh survived a no-confidence vote in the Indian Parliament, the IAEA approved the safeguard agreement, and the 45-nation NSG granted its waiver. Later that same year, the US Congress approved the deal, and the two countries officially signed it on October 10, 2008.

How did this happen? Which side subordinated its demands and accepted the other side's logic? Who made the courageous concession? It turns out *no one* did.

So *did* the 123 Agreement signed by the United States and India restrict nuclear tests? Did it stipulate the termination of nuclear commerce if India detonated a nuclear device? No one could say for sure.

On October 1, 2008, US Secretary of State Condoleezza Rice gave testimony to the Senate in which she declared, "Let me reassure you that an Indian test, as I have testified publicly, would result in most serious consequences. Existing US law would require automatic cutoff of cooperation, as well as a number of other sanctions, if India were to test."[4]

On the other side, on October 3, 2008, Indian External Affairs Minister Pranab Mukherjee, when asked whether India had sacrificed the right to test, clarified that "we would not like to convert this voluntary moratorium into a treaty-bound obligation. That position has been maintained."[5]

What is going on? What does the agreement actually say? If anyone ought to know, it would be Secretary Rice and Minister Mukherjee, the two people who signed the final agreement on October 10, 2008. The fact is that the 123 Agreement, and the network of agreements on which the US–India deal is structured, are deliberately vague. But the lack of precision is by design: this is the art of *strategic ambiguity*.

STRATEGIC AMBIGUITY

Strategic ambiguity is a risky tactic that can pay dividends when used at the appropriate time in the appropriate way. It is risky because it creates an agreement that can be interpreted differently by different parties—we will revisit this problem shortly. But multiple interpretations can also be valuable. This is because sometimes the problem isn't that the two sides cannot live with each other's demands, but that writing down or announcing *explicitly* what you're willing to live with is too problematic.

In this case, negotiators in the United States and India understood that any agreement, no matter what language was used to write it down, would involve both sides knowing that if India tested another weapon, which of course it *could* technically do, the United States would be forced to terminate the agreement due to domestic and international pressure. It really did not matter what was or was not in the signed agreement. The practical reality was that there was no way to stop India from testing a nuclear weapon if it wished, and there was no way to stop the United States from pulling out of the agreement if India tested. Knowing this would be the American reaction was the best incentive for India not to test a weapon in the first place. In other words, incentives were aligned and everyone in the room agreed on everything—there was no misunderstanding. Yet, putting the deal in writing would be problematic. For weeks negotiators labored over how to draft language that would be acceptable to each side given its constraints. Any language akin to "if India tests a nuclear weapon . . ." was a nonstarter in India; the absence of such language was unacceptable in the United States. The eventual solution was an approach that runs contrary to the instincts of most lawyers: the agreement had to be sufficiently *imprecise*, allowing each side to interpret the agreement and present it to its constituency in the most favorable way.

When neither side is willing to openly subordinate its demands on key issues or principles, strategic ambiguity—language that is deliberately open to multiple interpretations—can help the parties reach an agreement.

AMBIGUITY IS DANGEROUS IF THERE ARE NO INCENTIVES FOR APPROPRIATE BEHAVIOR

To appreciate the role of strategic ambiguity in the negotiator's tool kit—and to help draw some clear boundaries on when it is advisable—we need to first distinguish between different kinds of strategic relationships. There are those in which one or both parties have the incentive and ability to exploit the other—and will do so—*unless a contract or treaty makes this impossible or extremely costly*. In such a case, it is wise to have an agreement that clearly delineates the rights and responsibilities of each side and clarifies what behaviors are proscribed. Strategic ambiguity should be avoided in these instances. In contrast, there are relationships in which mutual interests are aligned enough so that the relationship is self-sustaining *regardless of what you write down*. Here, you have the flexibility to keep the contract incomplete or ambiguous if doing so helps you solve other problems (e.g., optics). In other words, strategic ambiguity should be limited to situations where other mechanisms are in place to enforce appropriate behavior from each party. India's External Minister Pranab Mukherjee made it quite clear that the nuclear negotiations fit this criterion—that is, that the deal was inherently self-enforcing based on each side's rights and interests—when he said, days before the signing of the agreement: "We have the right to test; others have a right to react."[6] This is not the kind of language that could go into the agreement but was perhaps suitable for a domestic audience. More generally, when the shadow of the audience looms large, people are sometimes willing to accept certain de facto limitations being imposed on them in a strategic relationship, but are unwilling to acknowledge or substantiate these in writing.

Strategic ambiguity should be used only when other mechanisms are in place to ensure compliance with appropriate behavior.

THE ROLE OF STRATEGIC AMBIGUITY IN EARLY RELATIONSHIPS

Strategic ambiguity can also be useful, ironically, when there is too little trust at the outset for the parties to reach a comprehensive agreement. Instead, parties may reach an initial deal that is incomplete or ambiguous, but which helps them stay engaged until trust is built. For example, in cross-cultural deal making, if a party fears that tying their hands with a long-term relationship is too risky, given the lack of a partner's prior track record, they will avoid signing a deal that is too committal. But being explicitly noncommittal may also muddy the waters. For instance, consider a situation in which Company X is sourcing from a new manufacturer, Company Y, but is unwilling to commit to a multiyear contract or make any other commitments to offset Company Y's investment in the deal. Company Y can live with the reality that, at the end of the day, if Y does not deliver a great product, X will look elsewhere. And yet, an agreement that is explicitly noncommittal, with numerous provisions that delineate all of the ways in which X is not responsible for the fate of Y, could send a very negative signal or force the parties to confront and get caught up haggling on issues that cannot be easily resolved. Introducing some degree of ambiguity regarding the nature of the relationship and the strength and length of commitment can provide both parties with the flexibility and freedom they need to overcome initial hesitations and pursue early-stage collaboration with the comfort of "no strings attached." Even when both sides will benefit from behaving appropriately, some arrangements remain easy to understand and agree to in principle, but are difficult to write down with precision, especially at the outset of what might be a long-term, evolving relationship.

Strategic ambiguity can help parties initiate relationships when there is insufficient trust for full commitment, but where being explicitly noncommittal is unacceptable.

It is worth highlighting that in each of the situations we've considered, strategic ambiguity is not meant to *substitute* for a genuine and durable understanding between the two sides. If there are deep divisions on key issues of substance, strategic ambiguity not only will fail to help but may make matters worse. This is the topic we now visit in more detail, as we consider the potential misuse of framing to resolve conflict.

5

THE LIMITS OF FRAMING

Charting a Path to War in Iraq

IN 2002, THE US government, under President George W. Bush, was pushing for a United Nations Security Council Resolution that would put the Iraqi government, under Saddam Hussein, in material breach of previous resolutions pertaining to, among other issues, Iraq's weapons of mass destruction (WMD) program. All parties agreed that weapons inspectors would go to Iraq to assess whether Iraq was now complying with UN demands. A strong disagreement surfaced when it came to next steps. The United States, along with the United Kingdom and others, demanded that a United Nations "authorization of force" against Iraq be automatically triggered in the event that Iraq failed to quickly satisfy inspectors. France, along with Germany, Russia, and others (including the inspectors themselves), wanted to give the inspectors more time and—crucially—did not want an automatic trigger for the use of force.[1] Instead, they demanded that the parties agree to meet again if the authorization of force seemed necessary. From the French coalition perspective, an automatic trigger almost guaranteed war even if there were no WMD program in place. The thinking was: How was Iraq to "immediately, unconditionally, and actively" prove the nonexistence of something that others believed the Iraqis were good at hiding and likely to lie about?

At the heart of the negotiation, then, was disagreement over a substantive issue (the trigger) that necessitated some type of compromise. More importantly, there was a deeper underlying dispute regarding the conditions under which the use of force would be appropriate.

A CAUTIONARY TALE

Rather than resolving this core dispute, the parties opted for a strategically ambiguous solution: UN Security Council Resolution 1441 did not contain *any* automatic triggers per se, but its language would allow the United States and its coalition partners to later interpret it as being sufficient to authorize the use of force.[2] For example, while making it clear that further deliberation would precede military action, it also stated that Iraq was being given "a final opportunity to comply with its disarmament obligations." Moreover, as the US Ambassador to the UN, John Negroponte, pointed out soon after Resolution 1441 was adopted, the trigger was not the *only* thing the resolution did not contain:

> If the Security Council fails to act decisively in the event of further Iraqi violations, this resolution does not constrain any Member State from acting to defend itself against the threat posed by Iraq or to enforce relevant United Nations resolutions and protect world peace and security.[3]

As long as both coalitions were on the same page regarding their assessments of Iraq's compliance with this resolution, there would be no problem: both sides could look forward to a second vote to authorize force if and when needed. Unfortunately, it was not long before the two coalitions disagreed about the extent of Iraq's compliance, and whether and how soon the use-of-force vote should be taken. Given the unresolved underlying dispute on this core issue, it became clear that the French and the Russians were not in favor of quickly resorting to force and would veto any such authorization. Meanwhile, for the Bush administration in the United States, which continued to favor the use of force, a failed authorization vote would be worse than no vote at all.

And so it transpired that, *without* a second vote on the use of force, *against* the strenuous objections of the French-led coalition, and even in the *absence* of any trigger for the use of force in the resolution, the US-led coalition went to war against Iraq on March 20, 2003. And *both* sides—the French and the United States—argued that they were acting in accordance with Resolution 1441. The failure of this approach to deal making can be seen not only in terms of the failure to prevent war, but because it led to even greater divisions and mistrust in the UN Security Council and beyond. Even if war was inevitable (for example, if the United States was committed to this course of action), the use of strategic ambiguity to gloss over deep divisions did not help and actually made matters worse.

AMBIGUITY IS NOT A REMEDY FOR SUBSTANTIVE CONFLICT

Ideally, ambiguity should be employed only if it helps to reach a deal that *all sides understand and accept substantively*, but which they are having difficulty writing down explicitly, due to the burden that is sometimes imposed by excessive precision. Unfortunately, even when there is no underlying agreement on substance, parties sometimes opt for strategic ambiguity simply because it is a convenient way to overcome a deadlock, or because it allows them to reach "some sort of agreement" rather than no deal. This is problematic because it only postpones the substantive conflict by sweeping it under the rug while creating a false belief that a worthwhile deal has been reached. When the conflict reemerges, it can be even worse because of dashed expectations, perceptions of breach, and the costly accumulation of psychological, political, or economic investments that parties have since made on the basis of their alleged agreement.

Ambiguity should not be used as a substitute for genuine agreement on substance.

A TRADE-OFF BETWEEN CURRENT AND FUTURE CONFLICTS

Strategic ambiguity involves a trade-off between minimizing current conflict and minimizing future conflict. If you are trying to reduce the likelihood of a dispute arising in the future, strategic ambiguity is not a good idea. The agreement should be as explicit and unambiguous as possible to avoid multiple interpretations of the deal as you go forward. If, however, you are more concerned about how to resolve current deadlock so that it does not obstruct deal making at the outset of the relationship, then one solution is to use strategic ambiguity. From this perspective, strategic ambiguity entails a bet—we accept a greater risk of future problems in exchange for making things easier for ourselves now. As we have seen, deciding whether to take the bet requires careful consideration of the costs and benefits, but a good rule is to lean away from strategic ambiguity when there are deep divisions on substantive issues that are unlikely to go away (or are likely to get worse) with the passage of time.

Ambiguity involves a trade-off between solving current conflicts and minimizing future conflicts.

BEWARE THE TEMPTATION TO SHAKE HANDS WHEN THERE IS NO AGREEMENT

As the Resolution 1441 negotiation demonstrates, parties often embrace strategic ambiguity with insufficient regard for the impact it can have on future conflict. This may be due to strategic myopia—that is, insufficient consideration of downstream consequences—but it can also result from incentive systems. If negotiators are rewarded for reaching a deal or punished for failing to do so, they will find a way to reach an agreement, however flawed. These incentives may be explicit, as they are in the business world, or implicit, as they might be in politics. When it is easier for the audience (e.g., voters, top management, media) to judge *whether* a deal was reached, and much harder to evaluate its long-term consequences, negotiators are likely to favor strategies that defuse current conflicts, even if doing so increases the likelihood or the magnitude of future conflicts.

If closing deals is rewarded, negotiators might conceal substantive disagreements to push through flawed deals.

AMBIGUOUS AGREEMENTS MAY BE PARASITIC

In fairness, there is another—more cynical—way to assess what transpired between the United States and France in 2003. Consider what would have happened if instead of a strategically ambiguous 1441, the United States and the French had just agreed to reach no deal. In all likelihood, this would have meant that the United States would act without

UN authorization—that is, go to war against Iraq with a handful of coalition partners, which is what it did anyway. So why bother reaching a deal at all? The reason for the deal may have been that both sides preferred an ambiguous agreement *that they knew would likely cause future conflict* over reaching no deal: the United States wanted to be able to claim UN authorization even though few countries were ever going to join in the attack, and the French wanted to avoid establishing precedents where the Security Council is completely sidelined when UN members want to go to war.

The cynical perspective suggests that, in fact, strategic ambiguity *did* serve the interests of both sides in this case and there was no deep disagreement on substance—that is, the French and the United States knew all along that the United States would act without broad UN support, but both wanted to feed the illusion that the UN had not been abandoned. This would give the United States some degree of legitimacy for its actions, and give the French some degree of legitimacy for the UN.

If this view is accurate, then the failure here is not the inappropriate use of strategic ambiguity from the point of view of the parties who were present in the negotiation—each of them succeeded in achieving its goals. The failure is at a system level, suggesting that sometimes, when negotiators at the bargaining table find a way for each side to declare victory, it is *not* in the service of the greater good, but rather to achieve their own narrow goals, perhaps at significant cost to other stakeholders. We refer to such behavior—that is, action designed to benefit everyone in the room at the expense of parties who are not at the table—as *parasitic value creation*.[4] The value captured by those at the bargaining table is "parasitic" in that it does not result from synergies or mutual benefit created through cooperation and trade; it comes out of the pockets of others.

Unfortunately, strategic ambiguity as a tool to "make everyone happy" can be effective in the hands of people who are actually creating no value in aggregate, but who will personally benefit from getting a deal done. The lesson, then, is especially important for stakeholders who may be at the receiving end of future negative consequences: beware of ambiguity or incompleteness in agreements that are sold to you. If substantive disputes will persist, or if costs will be incurred by other stakeholders—which you may need to work hard to discover if you were not privy to the discussions—you may want to demand greater clarity or precision in the deal, or a more robust explanation for why it should be done.

> ***Ambiguous or incomplete agreements might be parasitic, meeting at-the-table interests at the expense of other stakeholders.***

Having reflected on potential problems with using strategic ambiguity and, more generally, the considerations that should accompany any use of framing to resolve conflicts, it is important to note that in most cases, the use of framing helps overcome deadlocks *without* imposing the types of negative consequences seen in this chapter. It is also worth remembering that negotiation frames will *always* exist, regardless of whether someone has tried to influence them. There is inevitably some default lens through which proposals and options are being evaluated. The question is whether and how a negotiator might reframe a situation to achieve better or fairer outcomes for *all* parties—those who are at the table as well as others who are affected by the negotiation.

We have discussed at great length how a proposal or outcome can be framed. Let's end this section by zooming out and discussing the frame of the relationship itself. How parties perceive each other can have broad, powerful, and long-lasting effects on negotiations. If you are mindful of this, you will act early to create the right frame for the future relationship.

6
FIRST-MOVER ADVANTAGE

The Unbroken Peace Treaty

CAN YOU NAME THIS country? The longest standing treaty in United States history is with this country. The first building on foreign soil ever acquired by the United States is located there—and that building is also the only place outside of the United States to have ever been designated a National Historic Landmark.[1] This country has been a prominent supporter of the United States in its "war" against terrorism, but military cooperation between the two is not a recent development—soldiers from this country fought alongside American forces in World War I, and it emphatically sided with the United States in its fight against the Confederate states during the American Civil War. Likewise, the United States has long championed this country's aspirations for noninterference by foreign powers. It is also one of the 20 countries around the world with which the United States of America has a Free Trade Agreement. Which country is it?

Some more hints: It is in Africa. Approximately 99% of the population is Arab or Berber, and 99% is Muslim. It is one of only two countries on the continent that has been designated a "major non-NATO ally" of the United States, affording it special military and financial cooperation. Any other guesses?

Final hint: One of the greatest American films—with perhaps the most highly acclaimed screenplay—is set in the largest city of this country. Who is this special friend to America?

Historians and movie buffs who have seen *Casablanca* might have an advantage in identifying the African nation as being the Kingdom of Morocco. The real question, however, is what accounts for this long-lasting relationship?

WITHOUT MONEY OR MUSCLE

In 1786, Thomas Jefferson and John Adams signed the "Moroccan-American Treaty of Friendship" that had been negotiated between the American representative, Thomas Barclay, and Mohammed III, Sultan of Morocco.[2] The treaty, written in Arabic and then translated into English, had 25 articles, mostly pertaining to naval and commercial matters. The final article set the length of the treaty obligations: "This Treaty shall continue in full Force, with the help of God for Fifty Years." Almost 230 years later, it is still in effect. The treaty's preamble had been much more optimistic—and ultimately more accurate—when it stated that the agreement was made (according to the Islamic calendar) "on the twenty-fifth day of the blessed Month of Shaban, in the Year One thousand two hundred, *trusting in God it will remain permanent*."

But the signing of the Treaty of Friendship merely formalized a relationship that had already existed between the two countries for almost a decade. The first, and most consequential, step towards friendship was planted in 1777, when Morocco became *the first sovereign country* to recognize the independence of the fledgling United States of America. In December of that year, seeing the value of enhanced commercial relationships with America, the sultan announced that the ports of his country would be open to the United States. While it took a few years for the US government to respond to this offer—they had more pressing concerns during the war with England— it planted the seed that would grow into a friendship and a commercial relationship for centuries.

FIRST-MOVER ADVANTAGE

As we have seen previously, there is a powerful *first-mover advantage* when it comes to framing. The sooner a frame takes hold, the more likely it is to stick and to shape subsequent negotiations. We saw this when discussing default options: it pays to start with your initial template for the negotiations, or with your draft of the agreement. In the case of the longstanding relationship between the United States and Morocco, the friendship frame was set early on, when there was no prior, dominant frame to contest it. In business contexts, multiple frames are usually established very early in the deal-making process. These include, for example, who is perceived as strong or weak, whether it makes sense to be transparent or to be guarded, and which reference points or precedents are appropriate when evaluating offers, valuations, and so on. Effective negotiators are mindful of the influence such frames will have as the negotiation unfolds and seek to establish the preferred frame as early as possible.

There is a powerful first-mover advantage in framing. Whenever possible, seek to control the frame of the negotiation at the start.

REFRAME AS EARLY AS POSSIBLE

Because you do not always get to set the initial frame, you might need to act quickly to assess and change the frame as needed. Not so long ago, a very successful interventional cardiologist I know was negotiating a contract renewal with his hospital. He knew the hospital CEO understood the tremendous value he brought to the hospital and assumed this would be a smooth process. To his surprise, the CEO of the hospital began the negotiations with an aggressive opening offer that would *lower* his salary by 20%. The CEO justified this using data and extensive documentation that showed the hospital was losing money and that the doctor, too, was operating at a loss. Conveniently, the CEO had included all manner of hospital fixed costs in the calculations to make the case and had ignored various other ways in which the doctor was contributing to the bottom line and to other goals of the hospital system. Each time they met to discuss the situation, the conversation would get bogged down in intractable arguments over what constituted fairness and the legitimacy of specific line items in the CEO's profit/loss analyses.

It became clear to the doctor that the only way to dislodge the dominant "We are losing money so it is only fair that you should be paid less" framing would be to introduce an entirely different template as the basis for discussion. Before the next meeting, the doctor asked the CEO whether, given fairness was the concern, he would be open to an objective, third-party analysis of the fair market value of his contribution to the hospital. Many hospitals use comparative analyses in a region to decide on physician salaries, and there are firms that provide such services. The CEO agreed to this approach. When the data came in, it revealed, as the doctor had expected, that he was currently underpaid given the revenue he was generating for the hospital. Not only did this shift the conversation towards the appropriate *increase* in salary; also it gave the CEO the justification he would need to approve a salary increase for the doctor.

If the existing frame is disadvantageous, seek to reframe as soon as possible.

DISPUTES ARE EASIER TO PREEMPT THAN TO RESOLVE

One element that sets the Morocco example apart from earlier cases we have examined is that the initiatives by the sultan were not aimed at resolving an existing deadlock or dispute with the United States; rather, he was engineering a path that might preempt future conflicts. Just as early framing is more powerful than late framing, it is much easier to preempt a deadlock than it is to resolve one. This principle holds not only when it comes to managing grand strategic initiatives, but also in dealing with more parochial tactical issues.

Here is an amusing example that makes the point. At the Third UN Conference on the Law of the Sea (1973–1982), Tommy Koh, Singapore's permanent representative to the United Nations, chaired one of the key committees related to the contentious issue of deep seabed mining. With delegates from over 150 nations at the table, Ambassador Koh needed to find some way to reconcile the divergent interests and perspectives of everyone in the room. Discussing every issue with such a large group would have been impossible, so Koh needed some way to shrink the group to a more manageable number. This would not be easy to do if everyone felt that they had a right and reason to be there. Tommy Koh reflected on this issue, years later:

> In the case of the negotiation on the financial terms of mining contracts, we began in a room of 150 countries, and it was necessary to have meetings with 150 countries because you

> are indulging in public education . . . on what are the issues, what are the parameters, what are the various scenarios, [and to] explain to them all of the technical terms. . . . Once that's accomplished, you have to make a transition from this huge plenary group to a smaller forum. . . .[3]

But how do you exclude anyone, even when it is for the good of the whole group? Here's what Koh did:

> So I invented a new group called the "Group of Financial Experts," and I picked a meeting room that could accommodate maximum 40 people. It was open-ended—nobody's name. Anybody could come. But just by calling it the Group of Financial Experts was sort of intimidating. So a lot of my colleagues felt that they didn't qualify to join this group. I didn't try to dissuade them [by telling them] that they did. And so most people did not come. . . . And it gave us—in a smaller forum—[the ability] to advance the collective knowledge about the problem.

As we see in Koh's approach, effective negotiators try to foresee deadlock and create conditions that will allow people to walk away from direct confrontation without feeling that they are losing or conceding anything of importance. It would have been much harder to ask people to leave the room than it was to create a frame that dissuaded them from entering in the first place. It is a reminder to not wait for conflict to erupt before we start thinking about framing, optics, audience problems, and strategic ambiguity. If the parties are on a collision course, it is better to help them steer away from each other rather than to pick up the pieces afterwards.

A colleague and I recently discussed the following situation: a person was to be selected to oversee a peace process between warring factions within an ethnic group. We knew that the leader of one particular faction would feel strongly that he should be chosen because, from his point of view, he was *the* legitimate leader of the ethnic group and deserved to hold this esteemed position. The problem was that not all of the warring factions agreed, and this discrepancy was one of the key reasons for much of the infighting. This leader was too powerful to rebuff and too controversial to include.

From our point of view, we needed someone who could be trusted by all of the parties. My suggestion was for us to reframe and redefine the role of overseer so that it no longer represented prestige or status—and to do so before discussing the role in any detail with the parties. If the role were conceptualized as more bureaucratic and low-level, the leader would be less likely to fight for it.

Disputes are easier to preempt than to resolve. Decisions can sometimes be framed in ways that help people avoid confrontation in the first place.

HIGH-LEVERAGE MOMENTS FOR FRAMING

Both the Morocco example and the Law of the Sea scenario serve to highlight another commonly overlooked factor in negotiations: along with the big issues and decisions that parties must often confront, there are many less visible, less urgent, and seemingly simpler decisions that can sometimes have a large effect on the outcome of the deal. In Koh's case, given the enormity of the overall negotiation, the decision to move from a plenary group to a working group was not a particularly noteworthy moment. In the sultan's case, there was no urgency in reaching out to the United States, or in moving quickly to establish peaceable relations. In both cases, however, potential conflict was preempted by small, early actions that took place before there was a *need* to act.

This is not to suggest that one needs to worry about every small decision in a negotiation, but there are some small but consequential choices in most negotiations that deal makers should take seriously. I think of these as *high-leverage moments* in a negotiation—for relatively little effort, they allow you to significantly impact the frame and, as a result, the likelihood of success. These high-leverage moments tend to emerge in the early stage of the negotiation or relationship when the frame is still up for grabs and every decision has the potential to be imbued with heightened significance. This is powerfully demonstrated in an incident that dates back to the start of US–Morocco relations.[4] When Thomas Barclay was negotiating the treaty with the Moroccans, the sultan raised the issue of a tribute—a gift—which he said he ought to receive to secure the deal between the two countries. Barclay responded that the only "tribute" he could offer was a friendship with the United States on equal terms. If that was unacceptable to the sultan, Barclay said, he would have to go back to the United States without a treaty. In that small moment of high leverage, the sultan conceded and agreed to *a relationship based on equality*. That was a pretty smart move with a country that would go on to become the world's greatest superpower.

Early actions can take on heightened significance. Look for low-cost opportunities to powerfully influence the frame and to establish the appropriate expectations and precedents for the relationship.

SUMMARY OF LESSONS FROM PART I: THE POWER OF FRAMING

- Control the frame of the negotiation.
- Make it easier for the other side to back down from strong positions.
- Wise concessions on style and structure can help avoid costly concessions on substance.
- Pay attention to the optics: how will the deal look to the other side's audience?
- Help the other side sell the deal to their audience.
- Make it safe for the other side to ask for help on optics.
- Avoid one-issue negotiations: add issues or link separate one-issue negotiations.
- Negotiate multiple issues simultaneously, not sequentially.
- Diffuse the spotlight so one issue does not become too prominent.
- If there is only one issue, try splitting it into two.
- Unmask the underlying interests: incompatible demands can hide reconcilable interests.
- Be firm on substance, flexible on structure: I know where I need to get, I'm flexible on how I get there.
- Getting unstuck is a worthy enough short-term goal.

- Address the logic of appropriateness: what does a person like me do in a situation like this?
- Leverage social proof to boost appropriateness.
- Framing an option as unique is a double-edged sword.
- Frame your proposal as the default option.
- The party that drafts the initial version of the agreement or process gains leverage.
- Establish a proper reference point for their evaluations.
- Always justify your offer, but don't apologize for it.
- Strategic ambiguity can help resolve deadlock when no one can back down.
- Strategic ambiguity should be used only if other mechanisms are in place to ensure compliance.
- Strategic ambiguity can help overcome initial hesitations to starting relationships.
- Ambiguity is not a remedy for substantive conflict.
- Ambiguity involves a trade-off between current conflicts and future conflicts.
- If closing deals is rewarded, negotiators might conceal substantive disagreements to push through flawed deals.
- Ambiguous deals may be parasitic, hurting those who are not at the table.
- Be the first mover: control the frame early.
- If the existing frame is disadvantageous, reframe as early as possible.
- Better to preempt conflict than to resolve it: frame decisions in ways that help people avoid confrontation.
- Early in the relationship, find low-cost opportunities to create the right frame for the relationship.

Part II
THE POWER OF PROCESS

The good news is, there is light at the end of the tunnel. The bad news is, there is no tunnel.

SHIMON PERES

7

THE POWER OF PROCESS

Negotiating the US Constitution

THE WAR FOR AMERICAN independence between the United States and Great Britain lasted eight years, formally ending in the Treaty of Paris, which was signed in 1783. By that time, the Articles of Confederation had served as the governing document of the United States for six years.[1] By design, the Articles gave little power to the central government, and the sovereignty of the 13 states was paramount. The Articles went so far as to clarify that the relationship between the states was merely a "league of friendship with each other." This was to be expected given the confederation was formed by people who had just freed themselves from the grip of power vested in a distant monarch. Soon enough, however, problems with this arrangement emerged. George Washington, commander in chief of the Continental Army, had seen the failings firsthand during the war itself. Congress had no power to tax, and the states were often unwilling to contribute the funds necessary to pay military wages or the war debt owed to foreign countries. After the war ended, matters worsened. Congress was considered so powerless that its delegates often failed to even show up; on occasions when a quorum was reached, little was accomplished. Even bills aimed at raising tax dollars to pay the war debt were defeated, not because a majority of the states dissented, but because the Articles gave every state a veto. In 1786, Rhode Island defeated such a bill despite support in 12 other states; in 1787, New York cast the deciding vote to do the same.

Evidence that the Articles had serious shortcomings mounted. In 1787, the highly publicized but short-lived Shays' Rebellion, an uprising among Massachusetts farmers who had economic grievances, made the economic and political problems plaguing the young nation especially vivid. Soon after, the various states agreed to send delegates to the Constitutional Convention in Philadelphia. The goal of the convention was explicitly modest: to consider modifications to the Articles of Confederation. Had the convention been seen as an event at which reformers would try to completely overhaul the government and wrest power away from the states, it is unlikely that any state would have even sent delegates. Yet, that is precisely what occurred.

Although it is certainly possible to overstate the role any one person plays at historic events, James Madison is quite rightly considered to have been one of the few indispensable characters in Philadelphia that summer. Yet, by almost any measure, the deck was stacked against him. At 5 feet 4 inches, and weighing close to 100 pounds, Madison did not project strength or stature. Far from being a captivating orator, he was shy and sometimes spoke too quietly in the debates to be properly heard. At 36 years of age, he was neither a war hero, nor a prominent national figure, nor even a senior member of the delegation from his home state of Virginia. Most problematic, there was very little support for a significant overhaul among the American population at large, and the notion that state legislatures would accept any sizable reduction in their powers was almost unthinkable. Nonetheless, in large part due to Madison's efforts, when the convention ended, the delegates had drafted an entirely new constitution that shifted considerable power towards a new central government. By late 1788, the required supermajority of states (nine of 13) had ratified it, and by early 1789, the US Constitution became the law of the land. How did this happen?

NEGOTIATING THE IMPOSSIBLE

For his contributions, Madison would come to be known as the "Father of the Constitution." And while he spoke over 200 times during the debates that took place in the summer of 1787, much of what he managed to accomplish might be attributed to what took place *before* most other delegates even arrived in Philadelphia. By the time the convention started, Madison had already shaped the deliberations that would take place.[2]

Madison arrived in Philadelphia on May 3, 1787, 11 days before the Constitutional Convention was scheduled to start. True to character, he was the first delegate to show up. George Washington, a fellow Virginian—and the most popular man on the continent—would be the second to arrive ten days later. When Madison and Washington visited the convention hall on May 14 for the scheduled commencement of the now-historic deliberations, they discovered that apart from some local Pennsylvanians, they were the only two people from among the other 12 states to have made it to Philadelphia. While justifiably concerned by what the delay portended, Madison got straight to work. The task ahead, as Madison saw it, was to convince the other delegates that the Articles of Confederation needed to be thrown out completely. To be more precise, given the potentially fatal shortcomings of a system in which any one state could overrule all others on matters of national importance, the new system needed to vest significantly greater power in a national government.

Madison understood that the greatest barrier to the drastic change he wanted was the default process that was in place: the Articles of Confederation were going to be the starting point of any conversation. As long as the Articles served as the template to be revised, they would be too powerful an anchor in every discussion of how to structure government appropriately. A process based on, "How should we revise the Articles?" could never lead to as much change as a process based on, "What is the best system of government?" The process would need to be changed.

Madison, working with George Washington and other like-minded delegates from Pennsylvania and Virginia, started to draft an alternative document that could serve as the starting point for discussion. What came to be known as the "Virginia Plan" consisted of 15 resolutions that, although presented as revisions to the Articles, in fact upended the existing compact between the states. Among its proposals were the idea of proportional representation in Congress, giving power to citizens rather than state legislatures; the veto power of the executive branch; elements of checks and balances; and the ability of the legislative branch to negate state laws that were incompatible with the national interest. Perhaps most astutely, anticipating the resistance of state legislatures to the changes, it also proposed a revised process for ratifying the new Constitution: it called for ratification not by state legislatures, but by assemblies specifically selected for this purpose by the people of the various states.[3]

Not even the considerable talent gathered in Philadelphia in May 1787 could have created such a document without the exhaustive preparation Madison had undertaken before setting foot in Philadelphia. One month earlier, in April 1787, after countless weeks of careful and extensive research on the history of different forms of government dating at least as far back as ancient Greece, Madison had drafted a document titled "Vices of the Political System of the United States." In it, he laid out a careful critique of the existing system, as well as ideas on how the problems could be addressed. Shared with the Virginia and Philadelphia delegates in May, this treatise served not only as the backbone of the Virginia Plan but also as the basis for reformation presented at the Constitutional Convention.

The convention finally started on May 25. Only four days later, Virginia Governor Edmund Randolph presented the Virginia Plan. Reactions ranged from enthusiastic support to shock and anger. But the die was cast, and all of the debates to follow would take place in the shadow of the Virginia Plan. There was now an entirely new process in place; instead of debating the legitimacy of revisions to the Articles, arguments were focused on supporting or opposing elements of the Virginia Plan. Many compromises were made by all sides in the months ahead, but as each day progressed, the Articles of Confederation were left further behind.

HAVE A PROCESS STRATEGY

What truly exemplifies Madison's genius is not merely the extent of his preparedness, but the focus of it. Whereas most people know to prepare for the substantive discussions that will eventually occur, Madison understood the power of *shaping the process* that will ultimately determine whether, when, and how the substantive discussions will take place. The most obvious examples were Madison's extensive efforts in resetting the starting point of discussions and the coalition-building he did *before* the convention even started. If he had not executed these process interventions, the negotiations might well have gone a different way. Another crucial process element that favored Madison was the *gag rule* that delegates instituted to shield their debates from public interference; if too much information on the ongoing negotiations had leaked early on, it would have been difficult for some delegates to continue the controversial work of the convention. If these process elements had not been carefully considered and shaped, the debates would have started—and likely ended—quite differently.

The substance of a negotiation is about *what* the parties are trying to achieve. Process is about how they will get from where they are today to where they want to be. In the previous section, I discussed the peril of focusing exclusively on substance and ignoring the frame. In this section, I will make the same argument regarding process: even the most brilliant strategy for the substance of negotiations can be undermined if there is insufficient attention to process. Here are just *a few* elements of process to consider and try to shape:

- How long will negotiations last?
- Who will be involved and in what capacity?
- What will be on the agenda, and in what order will issues be discussed?
- Who will draft the initial proposal?
- Will negotiations be public or private?
- When and how will progress be reported outside of negotiations?
- Given multiple parties or issues, will there be one negotiation track or many?
- Will all the parties be in the same room at the same time?
- Will negotiations take place face-to-face or via technology?
- How many meetings will be scheduled?
- How will major deadlocks or other problems be managed?
- Will there be outside observers or mediators?

- Will deadlines, if any, be binding or not?
- What milestones might help build momentum and keep the process on track?
- If the negotiations end in no deal, when and how might parties reengage?
- Who are the parties that need to ratify the deal, and how much support is sufficient for passage?

In most negotiations, some or many of these factors will be predetermined, or there may be a default process in place due to precedent or the actions of other parties. But as we have seen, defaults need not be blindly accepted—they can be reset to great advantage. This happens only when negotiators have evaluated all of the important elements of process in advance and have assessed how alternative processes might facilitate or hinder progress.

Have a process strategy: how will you get from where you are today to where you want to be? Consider the factors that influence whether, when, and how substantive negotiations will occur.

DON'T IGNORE THE IMPLEMENTATION PROCESS

In the case of the United States Constitution, the crucial role of process can be seen even after the close of the convention. Much of the success in achieving *ratification* by the states can be attributed to the type of process that was implemented. Recall that many state governments would not have been in favor of the kinds of changes the new Constitution proposed. Moreover, many detractors of the Constitution were going to argue that delegates at the Constitutional Convention had exceeded their authority, that there was going to be too much power vested in the national government, and that individual rights were not sufficiently protected (a concern that was later remedied by the Bill of Rights).

How do you get sufficient support for a deal that is certain to shock many of those who have been outside of the negotiation? Fortunately for Madison and other supporters of the Constitution (dubbed the Federalists), the process for ratification was tailor-made to help them overcome opposition by the Anti-Federalists. First, and most crucially, according to Article VII of the Constitution, only nine of the 13 states needed to ratify the Constitution for it to go into effect for those states. This was despite the fact that any previous revision to the Articles of Confederation, which is what the new Constitution was supposed to be, had required a unanimous vote by all 13 states. Second, ratification took place through specially called state ratification conventions, rather than by the sitting state legislatures. Third, delegates were empowered to make only one choice—vote yes or no—and could not propose amendments or negotiate for revisions. And fourth, the Federalists moved quickly and strategically to schedule early votes designed to win passage in five of the pro-Constitution states. This made it easier for delegates in other states who might have been on the fence to feel more comfortable voting in favor. Certainly, substantive concessions were also made to shore up support in some states—most notably, reaching an understanding that the Bill of Rights would be taken up by the first Congress under the new Constitution. But it is hard to imagine how the Federalists could have achieved success without the right process elements in place. If ratification had required consensus, states like Rhode Island, which had not even sent delegates to the Convention, would have surely vetoed all efforts from the start. Had states been allowed to vote on different versions of the Constitution, or to reopen debates in the hopes of scoring concessions, deadlock would have almost certainly resulted. Likewise, had the Anti-Federalists been given more time to mount an organized challenge to the Constitution, things might have ended differently.

A process strategy for deal making is not enough—you also have to strategize the implementation process. What will be required for successful implementation? How will you garner sufficient support for the deal? How will you ensure ratification?

THE POWER OF PREPARATION

As evident throughout, Madison understood the power that comes from being the most prepared person in the room. It was this quality that inspired him to conduct his scholarly research before the convention and to reach out to other Virginia delegates asking them to arrive early to draft "some materials for the work of the Convention." He brought the same quality into the Convention itself. William Pierce, the delegate from Georgia who became famous for penning character sketches of other delegates, referred to Madison as someone who "always comes forward as the best informed Man of any point in the debate."

The benefits of thorough preparation are as evident in complex deal making as they are in board meetings, sales calls, legal proceedings, and promotion discussions in faculty meetings. In every one of these environments, some show up woefully unprepared, some have done enough preparation to get by, and others are ready to respond to almost anything. In a truly important situation, you don't want to be any of these people. You want to be a Madison: someone who has all of the facts at your fingertips, who can anticipate the arguments and reservations of the other parties, and who has carefully examined not just the strengths but also the weaknesses of your own argument. This is the person who is hardest to ignore or push around, to whom others are most likely to give deference, and who will most easily shape or reshape the process and the substantive negotiations effectively.

Be the most prepared person in the room. Know the facts, anticipate the arguments, and understand your weaknesses.

In the chapters that follow, we dig deeper into the importance of process and identify important principles to keep in mind as you navigate your own negotiations and conflicts. As we will see throughout this section, while getting the substance right is essential, getting the process wrong can still be fatal. Moreover, as the next chapter reveals, it is not enough to give process elements due consideration: process should be given *precedent*. Focusing on process early can sometimes help avoid deadlocks and ugly conflicts altogether.

8

LEVERAGING THE POWER OF PROCESS

Reneging on a $10 Million Handshake

SUN MICROSYSTEMS WAS STILL in its infancy when, in 1983, two of its cofounders set out to raise $10 million in funding.[1] After considering a number of options, Vinod Khosla and Scott McNealy had decided to pursue financing from a strategic investor, a Fortune 100 company that saw the benefit of getting access to the technology Sun was developing, and for whom the investment size would be nominal.[2] Sitting down with the Fortune 100 CEO, Khosla and McNealy reached an agreement: a $10 million investment on a post-money valuation of $100 million.[3] The parties shook hands on the deal and agreed to meet the following week in Chicago to finalize the term sheet.

Khosla and McNealy flew from San Francisco to Chicago for what they expected to be a short meeting to finalize remaining terms, most of which would entail standard provisions. They were surprised when the CEO showed up to the meeting with a dozen people, including a flock of bankers and lawyers. It was soon obvious that the bankers and lawyers would be doing the talking today, and that the negotiations would be conducted *de novo,* as if the discussions a week earlier had never taken place. As far as the investors were concerned, the investment size and the valuation were still entirely up for grabs.

Khosla and McNealy could only speculate as to what was happening. Had the CEO never perceived their "agreement" as being final? Were the bankers and lawyers simply trying to prove their worth by landing a better deal? Was there a perception across the table that Sun was too committed or desperate at this point to push back against last-minute demands?

The fact was, if push came to shove, Khosla and McNealy were willing to accept a lesser deal. But to accede to the demand for renegotiation would be costly—financially and on principle. What to do?

WITHOUT MONEY OR MUSCLE

Khosla recalls his plan of action: "I did not even want to ask them what numbers they had in mind. I did not want to go any further down that path. I wanted to make a stand right away on the process." Khosla told the group that his understanding was that certain terms had already been agreed to, and that he did not want to negotiate them again. Anticipating the possibility that the other side may not have expected this response, Khosla offered to give them time to regroup and discuss the matter. His message to them was essentially the following: "We had agreed on some things. Let's start there. If that's not what you want to do, then we need to discuss this relationship more fundamentally. Are we where we thought we were, or someplace else? Why don't you talk amongst yourselves and let us know: Have we agreed or not?"

The Sun cofounders left the room to allow the investors to deliberate. When they returned a few minutes later, they discovered that nothing had changed. From the other side's perspective, the numbers were still open for negotiation.

Now that the other side had doubled down on their hard-line strategy, Khosla and McNealy could think of no easy way to dislodge them. Perhaps they had reached the conclusion that last week's agreement was too generous. But it was also possible that the real problem was a lack of organization on the other side, or that no one was prepared to back down too quickly, especially in front of the CEO and the Sun team. This left two options as far as Khosla and McNealy could see. The first was to accept a hit on the numbers and just get the deal done. But Khosla and McNealy decided to take the second option; they told the CEO that they would love to continue discussions where they had left off the previous week, but if that was not possible today, they would have to leave Chicago without a deal.

About an hour later, Khosla and McNealy were on their way back to San Francisco with no deal. They then mustered up whatever resolve they had left to stop themselves from calling the CEO back after reaching home. If they had understood each side's interests well, the dollars involved should not have been a deal breaker for the other side. Khosla remembers: "Valuation mattered a lot to us. We just wanted the money at the best price, with the least dilution of our equity. Their interests were mostly strategic, and the numbers were not big for them. Losing the deal would hurt us but not kill us; and as far as we could tell, they did need us."

The cooling-off period worked. A few days later, the CEO called Khosla and agreed to go back to the original terms. This time around, when the teams met to finalize the deal, there were no surprises.[4]

NEGOTIATE PROCESS BEFORE SUBSTANCE

What had led to this conflict? In everything from mundane negotiations to complex deal making to protracted conflicts, I have often witnessed a tendency to rush towards achieving agreement on substance and to ignore alignment on process. Of course, both are necessary. But when it comes to important negotiations, process considerations should, in large part, precede substantive deal making: *negotiate process before substance.*

Consider the following: you have been negotiating with your counterpart for weeks. After considerable effort, you seem close to reaching a deal. You decide to offer one final concession that you have so far resisted and agree to one of their more onerous demands—a move you hope will seal the deal. You make the concession, and the other party responds, "Thank you. This is extremely helpful. I appreciate your flexibility. Now, I'd just like to go over things with my boss to see what she thinks about it." And you are sitting there, stunned, thinking to yourself: "What? You have a boss? I thought this was going to be the end. I have nothing more to give." The mistake, in this somewhat stylized example, is one that is all too common. It is a failure to negotiate process before diving into substance.

Negotiating the process involves evaluating the default (or proposed) process and reshaping it if necessary and possible. It also entails asking questions, sharing assumptions and expectations, and reaching as close to a common understanding as possible *on the path from where you are to the finish line.* How will we get from here to there, and what are the factors that can influence the trajectory and speed? A failure to negotiate process effectively can lead to mistakes on substance later on, including poorly timed concessions; ill-conceived proposals or demands; coordination failures across different tracks or channels in the negotiation; and the failure to anticipate barriers, such as deadlines, political or bureaucratic hurdles, and the behavior of spoilers.[5]

Negotiate process before substance. Understand and influence the process before diving too deeply into substantive discussions or concession making.

SYNCHRONIZE WITH THE OTHER PARTY ON PROCESS

Just because you've negotiated the process does not mean things cannot go wrong. Even when there is clear agreement on process at the outset, parties can sometimes get misaligned regarding their views on where they are in the process. For example, one party may feel that they are close to a deal and should forgo other options, while the other thinks it is still legitimate to be shopping around. In the case of Sun, the conflict was probably not as much about dollars and cents as it was about a lack of coordination on where they were in the process; indeed, no further concessions were needed for Sun to lock in the investment. Khosla still does not know what was really behind the seeming about-face by the CEO. But whether it was an attempt to squeeze a few last-minute concessions, or simply a difference of opinion as to whether the deal had really been reached a week earlier, one lesson is clear: it is important to align expectations regarding where you are in the process.

Misalignment on process can derail deals. Ensure—early and often—that there is agreement about what has been accomplished and what the path ahead looks like.

SEEK CLARITY AND COMMITMENT

So far we have been assuming that you have some ability to create a process that is to your liking, but this is clearly not always the case. In my experience, even when you have no ability to *shape* the process, there is much to be gained by seeking clarity and commitment on the process. Greater *clarity* (an understanding of the process) and *commitment* (assurances that the process will be followed) can help negotiators navigate towards better outcomes and avoid strategic and tactical mistakes even when they do not have the leverage to change the process.

The same is true in negotiations of all types. For example, if bankers are running the sale of an asset such as a company, they have a lot of choice and control over the negotiation or auction process they design (e.g., how many rounds of bidding, on what basis bidders will be eliminated, what information will be shared and when, etc.). If I am on the other side of the table, even if I have limited influence on their process strategy, it would be a mistake not to get as much clarity as possible on what the process will be and as much commitment as possible that it will not be altered to my detriment. Likewise, salespeople and strategic deal makers who don't fully investigate how a client organization makes buying or partnering decisions are putting themselves at an unnecessary disadvantage, even if there is no opportunity to influence the process. Even in simple situations, it is remarkable how often people will forgo the possibility of gathering process information that is both available and useful—for example, a job applicant failing to investigate how long an employer needs to make a hiring decision, or a homeowner not seeking clarity on how long a home renovation should take and what factors could cause delays.

Even if you cannot influence the process, seek to get as much clarity and commitment on it as possible.

NORMALIZE THE PROCESS

If you fail to negotiate or get clarity regarding the path ahead, you risk being blindsided later in the process. But it is not enough that *you* have clarity—*the other side* must have it as well. If they don't, you may be the one who suffers the consequences. How so? If you have ever witnessed or participated in a mediation process where there is a high degree of animosity between the disputing parties, you may have heard the mediator say something that is quite important in the initial meeting. A good mediator will, in one form or another, issue the following caveat early on in the proceedings:

> You think you hate each other today? We will be working together on some difficult issues in the coming weeks, and I can tell you from experience, about three days into this process, you are going to hate each other more than you've ever hated each other. And when that happens, I want you to remember something: that's normal.

Why would a mediator say this to disputing spouses, neighbors, business partners, or other antagonists? Consider what happens if the mediator fails to issue this warning. A few days into the process, the parties begin to struggle with rising tensions and the kinds of extreme emotions they had so far avoided by refusing to discuss serious problems. They might infer that things are getting worse, not better, and think, "This process is not helping!" They may even opt out of the process altogether. If, however, the mediator has told them ahead of time that it is *normal* to feel acute anxiety and emotions, and that difficult conflicts don't get resolved without hitting some new lows along the way, they are more likely to stick with the process.

The mediator's tactic is important for negotiators of all kinds. One of the most important things a negotiator can do, especially when the path ahead is likely to be difficult or unexpected, is to *normalize the process* for the other parties in the negotiation. Give them a preview of what to expect—the good and the bad—in the days, weeks, or years ahead. If you do not manage expectations in this way, the first time something goes wrong, they will question your intentions or capability, or doubt the viability of the process. I have seen this problem arise in everything from mismanaged sales cycles, to poorly handled early discussions between cofounders, to cross-cultural business negotiations, to negotiations between governments and armed insurgents. In every case, the negotiations were difficult enough on their own without the effects of mismanaged expectations. If you have normalized the process by clarifying what may delay or disrupt progress at times, which kinds of snags are inevitable (but remediable), and why things might depart from plan, the other side's reactions to these events will be more manageable.

Normalizing the process is important not only across the table but also with stakeholders on your own side. If you are taking calculated risks for future success, investing resources in plans that will pay off further into the future, or sacrificing immediate progress in preparation for a more comprehensive victory later, it is important to educate your stakeholders—investors, board members, employees, constituents, allies, the media, the public, fans, and so on—not only about what you're doing and why, but what the path *looks and feels like* between where you are today and where you plan to be. Even the wisest strategy is likely to have detractors, but negotiators often make life harder for themselves by failing to prepare stakeholders for the process they will need to endure.

Normalize the process. If other parties know what to expect, they are less likely to overreact to or overweight the significance of doubts, delays, and disruptions.

ENCOURAGE OTHERS TO NORMALIZE THE PROCESS FOR YOU

As important as it is to normalize the process for others, it is also important to have others normalize the process for you. It does neither side any good for predictable problems to go undiscussed. You are less likely to judge them harshly in the aftermath of adverse events if the other side has prepared you for the types of disruptions that are common when negotiating with people, organizations, cultures, or countries such as theirs. Moreover, in anticipation of some potential problems, you may be able to offer solutions that mitigate the likelihood of (or damage from) such events.

It is not always easy to get the other side to discuss these issues. The reason people often fail to be forthcoming about potential problems is that, early on, before the deal has been signed, everyone is in "selling" mode. Salespeople, job seekers, employers, corporate deal makers, diplomats, and anyone else hoping to get the other side to say "yes" to working together has an incentive to make it seem as if things will go smoothly. They do not want to spend too much time delineating all of the ways things can go poorly, lest this destroy any chance of winning the deal, especially if their competitors for the deal may not be as forthright. This is why some of the onus is on you to encourage an honest conversation about the kinds of things that could go wrong in the deal-making process. In my experience, the more credibly you can assure the other side that you have enough experience to know that every protracted negotiation and every meaningful relationship has disruptions—and that discussing the risk factors *enhances rather than diminishes your likelihood of consummating the deal with them*—the more likely it is that you will have a productive conversation that helps both sides in the future.

Encourage others to normalize the process for you—and make it safe for them to do so.

EVEN THE OTHER SIDE'S REFUSAL TO CLARIFY OR COMMIT IS INFORMATIVE

Of course, there is no guarantee that the other side will respond to your request for clarity or discuss potential problems that may arise, but even a refusal by the other side to answer certain questions can be informative. In the case of process, if the other party in the deal or dispute will not answer reasonable questions about process, it allows you to further explore whether this reflects bad intentions or a lack of preparation on their part, or that they are merely keeping their options open. At the very least, you can be more vigilant as you navigate the deal.

Asking for clarity and commitment is valuable even if the other party is unwilling to provide them. It is better to know there is a lack of commitment and to adapt accordingly than to incorrectly assume that the process will unfold as you hope.

MINIMIZING THE LIKELIHOOD THAT THE OTHER SIDE RENEGES

The other risk is that your negotiating partner *does* clarify and commit to a process and then still reneges on it. I don't know many seasoned negotiators who have not experienced this at some point. Yet, I have found that even in very difficult disputes, if people see value in preserving their credibility, they will often honor their word. Whether they follow through on their earlier assurances also depends on the extent to which the commitment they gave was made *personally, explicitly, unambiguously*, and *publicly*. More often, broken commitments are those that were (a) made by someone other than the person who is now reneging, (b) implied but never stated very explicitly, (c) stated in somewhat ambiguous terms, and/or (d) made behind closed doors. For this reason, whenever possible, it is useful to get commitments that address these features. Even a relatively well-intentioned party might be tempted to renege when incentives change and they can justify to themselves that they were not the ones to make the commitment, or that a lack of explicit statements of intent allows them to change their minds.

The risk of reneging is lower when commitments are personal, explicit, unambiguous, and public.

THEY RENEGED: WHEN AND HOW TO WALK AWAY

What if, despite your efforts, the other side reneges on their commitment? How should you handle a perceived violation of the process? While things worked out very well for Khosla and McNealy, is it really wise to call off negotiations when a process breach has occurred? Or, more precisely, when is it wise to push back? And how should you do it?

Sometimes, instead of walking away, the wisest move is to give the other side the benefit of the doubt, or to try to investigate and reconcile the diverging perspectives. You may discover, for example, that the other side really intended no breach, or that they are facing other pressures or constraints that make the breach necessary from their point of view. Other times, the breach is intended, or even premeditated, but you want to stay at the table because you have too much to lose by walking away or by escalating the conflict on the grounds of process impropriety.

Let's take a closer look at the Sun approach to identify some of the key considerations that should guide us when deciding whether to accept or challenge a perceived process breach. Why did it succeed? First, from the Sun perspective, there was a high degree of certainty that a deal had been reached the prior week and that the current behavior was inappropriate. Second, the Sun negotiators felt very comfortable in the value they brought to the table; they did not think they had to sweeten the deal substantively to make it worthwhile for the other party. Third, they offered a principle-based reason for cutting off the negotiations, being clear that it was not about the money per se, but about the respect for process commitments. Finally, the Sun negotiators did not simply walk away from the table; they clarified the conditions under which they would be willing to resume negotiations. One thing the Sun negotiators did not do, which I would have advised, was to try to give the other side a face-saving means of calling back and reengaging. It's best if you don't force the other side to choose between accepting your demands and saving face. Even small gestures can help in a case like this, such as offering to make the follow-up phone call, or offering a small concession on style or structure that gives the other side an excuse for changing their stance.

These are five very important elements to consider before disengaging on the basis of process conflict:

- Can we be sure it was a breach, or does the other side have reasons to see things differently?
- Do we bring sufficient value to the table, and does the other party understand this?
- Can we justify our actions on the basis of acceptable principles?
- Have we clarified what would be required to fix the breach?
- Have we given the other party a face-saving way to return to the table?

The more of these questions that you can answer in the affirmative, the easier it will be for you to successfully challenge a perceived process breach.

Before walking away due to a process breach, consider: (a) whether the other side considers it a breach, (b) how much each side loses, (c) how you will justify walking away, (d) whether they know how to remedy it, and (e) how they can do so without losing face.

FULL AGREEMENT ON PROCESS IS NOT ALWAYS POSSIBLE OR DESIRABLE

This does not mean that you should expect or even want the path forward to always be entirely mapped out. Sometimes the path is uncharted because of a lack of visibility at the outset, and it can be clarified only once substantive negotiations get under way. Other times, someone cannot or does not want to commit to a strict process because it limits flexibility. It is important to give these considerations the respect they deserve on both sides, and to make sure that the desire to pin down a clear and rigid process does not unnecessarily delay progress on substance. But process should never be entirely ignored. An effort must be made to ensure that everyone is moving, to the extent possible, in the same direction and at the same pace. Looking back to the lessons learned in the early days of negotiating for Sun, Khosla recalls:

> One of the things I now do differently is to pay much more attention to where each side thinks we are in the process. If I think we have an agreement but they don't, we get into trouble like we did in Chicago. That does not mean I always want to make everything explicit as soon as possible. Sometimes, for example, early on in negotiations when you are also pursuing other options, the right strategy may be to keep things implicit or informal, or to not even try to reach a mutual understanding. But in all cases, you need to think about where each side is in the process.[6]

Commitment to a rigid process is not always possible or advisable. If the process is flexible, make sure all parties understand the degree to which there is commitment.

Having considered the importance of negotiating process, it is worth looking at some of the reasons why the wrong process can take hold. For one thing, the process we have today may not be a choice, but a consequence of poor decisions that were made before the current conflict arose. Other times, even our well-intentioned attempts at creating the right process can backfire. The next chapter looks at how we might anticipate these potential problems and what principles might guide us when we confront them.

9

PRESERVE FORWARD MOMENTUM

Strikes and Lockouts in the NHL

WHAT'S THE DIFFERENCE BETWEEN a collective bargaining agreement (CBA) negotiation in the National Hockey League and open-heart surgery? One of them is long, painful, and expensive with no guarantee that you will fix the problem. The other is a well-established medical procedure.

As of this writing, it has been over 20 years since NHL owners and players succeeded in negotiating a CBA without a strike or a lockout that caused serious economic damage. (A strike is a player-initiated work stoppage; a lockout is when owners initiate the work stoppage.) At the beginning of the 2012–13 season, owners locked out players so that no games would be played until a deal was signed. By the time they reached agreement, roughly four months later, almost half of the games had been canceled for the season. A similarly lengthy lockout had done the same degree of damage during negotiations in the 1994–95 season. The award for worst negotiation in professional sports might have to go to the disastrous 2004–05 NHL season. That lockout lasted over ten months, and *every single game* of the season—all 1,230 of them—along with $2 billion in revenue, was lost because the two sides could not reach a deal. After each of these lockouts, the media has speculated as to who won and who lost. A pattern seems to have emerged: the owners often look like winners on the day the contract is signed, but as the complex contractual terms play out over the ensuing years, we usually find out the players actually did quite well.

It was not always so. The dispute in 1992 was an entirely different story. The work stoppage that year lasted only ten days, from April 1 to

April 11. When the dust settled, there was no debate: the players had gotten almost everything they had demanded. It was the shortest and most effective work stoppage in NHL history, perhaps in all of professional sports. What accounts for this difference? Why was this conflict so short-lived? Why did the players win so handily?

WITHOUT MONEY OR MUSCLE

The players were not better organized or more aggressive in 1992. Nor did they demonstrate special skills at the bargaining table. In fact, the outcome had almost nothing to do with *how* the two parties negotiated, and everything to do with *when* they negotiated. The one savvy—or fiendish, depending on your perspective—tactic the players used was choosing *not* to call for a strike at the start of the season in October, but to wait until it would be most harmful to owners. The season started with no signed CBA in place, but games continued while the owners and players negotiated. Then, as soon as the regular season ended and the playoffs were about to begin in April, the players walked out. This gave them tremendous leverage. Simply put, players earn paychecks throughout the season, but owners stand to make a disproportionate amount of their profits during the playoffs. With the playoffs held hostage, the cost of not reaching a deal was asymmetric; owners now had much more to lose. The result? The players got everything they asked for.

After being burned in 1992, the owners seem to have made sure they would never be caught in such a vulnerable position again. Every time a CBA has come up for negotiation since 1992, the owners have preemptively locked out the players at the start of the season.[1] This destroys tremendous value, all in the service of ensuring that both sides are losing money and owners are not the only ones having to make concessions. Waiting to strike before the playoffs may have seemed like a brilliant tactic in 1992, but it's the kind of tactic you can use exactly once. The 1992 strike, which was the first NHL work stoppage in 75 years,[2] created a destructive precedent that has been unbroken since.

PRESERVE FORWARD MOMENTUM

In protracted conflicts where finding a solution will take a long time—and in relationships where the parties will have to negotiate with each other again in the future—it is necessary to *preserve forward momentum.* Forward momentum is the deliberate, gradual progress towards eliminating obstacles and creating the conditions that might eventually lead to a successful outcome. Unfortunately, as seen in the NHL example, short-term temptations abound that create the risk of sacrificing forward momentum. The desire to "win" today can make it difficult to make even modest progress tomorrow.

There is nothing, per se, inappropriate about trying hard to get the best deal for one's constituents. The problem surfaces when this pursuit induces negotiators to break long-standing norms of behavior, to disrupt implied or explicit agreements, or to legitimize the use of "whatever it takes" tactics in an environment where cooperation and moderation might have otherwise taken root. Instead of doing whatever possible to make progress easier, negotiators who engage in such behaviors will motivate a desire for revenge and displace collaborative rules of engagement.

This happens not only in sports and politics, but all too often in business. It is easy to recall negotiators who have agreed to a deal only to renege on it and demand more when a better offer came along. In one case, a founder reached agreement and shook hands with a venture capitalist and then backed out when someone else threw a bit more money on the table. The VC held it against him for years and had no problem letting others in their relatively tight-knit industry know about it. I can think of other deal makers who took advantage of the other side's vulnerability early on in a relationship, thereby displacing the norm of fair play that might otherwise have taken hold.

The same happens in diplomacy. One of the major barriers to the resolution of armed conflict in Colombia, for instance, arose in the 1980s when the Revolutionary Armed Forces of Colombia (FARC) entertained the possibility of phasing out their brutal armed insurgency in favor of joining the political process. After some early signs of electoral success by the FARC-affiliated political party (the Patriotic Union), paramilitary groups and government-affiliated security forces killed off many hundreds of its members, candidates, and elected officials. In negotiations ever since, whenever the government demanded disarmament by the FARC prior to granting political participation, the latter balked, making it all the more difficult to create a process that would lead to disarmament. More generally, in such conflicts, short-sighted attempts at one-upmanship on both sides of the table—the violent suppression of relatively moderate opposition groups (perpetrated by governments), opportunistic terror attacks (perpetrated by insurgents), and human rights violations and cease fire violations (perpetrated by both)—have long-term consequences for whether and when the parties can reengage productively and make progress towards achieving peace. Undoubtedly, spoilers or extreme factions who oppose a diplomatic solution will often commit these acts. But they are also, too often, committed by those who *can* envision a negotiated peace but who sacrifice progress in the pursuit of short-term victories and advantage.

Preserve forward momentum. Before using tactics to gain advantage, consider: how will this affect our ability to negotiate productively in the future?

THE DARK SIDE OF CONSENSUS

Short-term greed is not the only reason negotiators sometimes sacrifice forward momentum. For example, in multiparty negotiations, even when intentions are benign, progress can be stymied if the group needs or desires consensus. Bringing everyone on board might be impossible, or prohibitively costly, and you may end up sacrificing the possibility of a viable deal in the pursuit of consensus. For example, in sports conflicts, there are not just two sides to the negotiation: big-market teams have different concerns than small-market teams, profitable teams have different interests than unprofitable teams, rookies have different interests than established players, and star players have interests that differ from those of average players. How do you ensure that everyone is happy with the outcome? When negotiating business partnerships, there will be people on the other side who value what you bring to the table highly, but also those who value it little, not at all, or even negatively. How likely are you to consummate a deal if anyone can block the partnership? Or, when a family is trying to organize a large reunion, or a couple is trying to make plans for a wedding, there may be many people who have or want a say in matters. It is worth thinking through whether it is wise to give everyone veto power.

Consensus certainly has its merits. There is something very appealing about having unanimous support for an agreement or decision. But the more people who have veto power, the fewer the degrees of freedom you have to structure a satisfactory deal, because there are too many demands on the limited resources available. The need to bring everyone on board creates a situation in which anything that isn't bolted down is subject to compromise, and the emergent agreement is likely to be strategically shortsighted—that is, designed to solve current problems at the cost of ignoring or exacerbating future problems. Recall that this was precisely the problem with the Articles of Confederation. Consensus also creates incentives for "hostage taking," as when someone knows that theirs is the final vote required and holds out for extreme concessions.

Consensus deals can be shortsighted. As the number of parties with veto power increases, the degrees of freedom for deal structuring decreases.

THE PRINCIPLE OF SUFFICIENT CONSENSUS

Because the pursuit of consensus can undermine progress and disrupt forward momentum, in large, multiparty negotiations, deal makers and diplomats will often try to adopt the principle of *sufficient consensus.* Instead of requiring that everyone at the table vote in favor of each proposal, the parties agree that negotiations can proceed as long as there is a "high enough" level of acceptance among and within the parties (e.g., 80% of all parties must agree in favor of the provision, and 60% of all individuals must agree). We see such an approach taken in everything from international climate deals, to peace processes, to the adoption of national constitutions. To avoid giving one or a few parties the ability to derail the process or to scuttle a final agreement, the requirement for progress and ratification needs to be lowered. A similar approach can make sense in corporate contexts. Consensus may be necessary and achievable in some circumstances, but when there is a high degree of conflict, leaders who make it clear that they want input and support, but do not require unanimity, are more likely to be able to implement ideas and avoid unhealthy inaction.

In complex deals and protracted conflicts, especially if hostage taking is a concern, a sufficient consensus approach can be more appropriate than seeking unanimity.

LOWER THE BAR FOR PROGRESS, RAISE THE BAR FOR AGREEMENT

What if the final agreement, for whatever reason, *must* be accepted by all parties? You can still safeguard forward momentum by using a sufficient-consensus process for all of the deliberations that will precede a final deal. In other words, when negotiating an interim agreement, or when drafting any individual provision of what will eventually be a final deal, "sufficient" support around the table is enough to move negotiations forward; at the end of the negotiation, all parties can still vote yes or no on the final, comprehensive deal that is reached. I have often advised the following when negotiating in contentious environments: *Keep a low bar for progress, but a high bar for final agreement.* This preserves momentum because it reminds people that although every person at the table is likely to find certain elements of the deal to be objectionable, or even abhorrent, these ought not to be showstoppers; it may be wise to continue the negotiation to see whether the final agreement is still preferable to no deal.

Keep a low bar for progress on individual elements of the deal, but a high bar for approving or ratifying the comprehensive final agreement.

NOTHING IS AGREED UNTIL EVERYTHING IS AGREED

Earlier we discussed the benefit of negotiating multiple issues simultaneously rather than negotiating one issue at a time. When there is limited trust, this allows both sides to ensure that their concessions in one area are being reciprocated in another. However, in especially complex negotiations, it is not always possible to discuss all of the important issues simultaneously. For example, in peace processes, the different issues (e.g., disarmament, economic reform, political participation) may be addressed months apart; in large international agreements, there may be separate channels to discuss different issues. Even in business deal making it is often the case that different elements of the deal will need to be negotiated by different people and at different times. One of the concerns negotiators will raise in such situations is that it is too risky to concede or even signal flexibility in one area when you do not know how other aspects of the deal will turn out. This way of thinking can bring progress to a halt. One partial solution to the problem is for all parties to explicitly agree to the principle of "nothing is agreed until everything is agreed." Accordingly, all sides acknowledge that nothing either side has said, implied, or proposed is irrevocable until a full agreement is reached. This gives people greater freedom to brainstorm different solutions and to experiment with being more conciliatory on parts of the deal, knowing that their right to retract any partial proposal or individual concession is protected by "until everything is agreed."

The principle of "nothing is agreed until everything is agreed" can help overcome paralysis by allowing people to make concessions safely.

THE COST OF TRANSPARENCY DURING THE BARGAINING PROCESS

A similar logic is at play when deal makers and diplomats decide to negotiate behind closed doors, allowing minimal transparency into the deliberations. As with consensus, transparency is beneficial for many reasons, but in the case of extremely difficult negotiations, transparency *during the bargaining process* often does more harm than good. It is hard enough for negotiators to reveal that they are willing to compromise when the discussion is private. If every statement, concession, or proposal will be made public before there is any guarantee that a final deal is possible, negotiators will be under tremendous pressure not to say anything that might be construed as weakness or betrayal. When you are negotiating the seemingly impossible, this is an added constraint that you cannot afford. It will stifle progress.

Instead, you usually want to give the negotiators as much privacy as possible during the bargaining phase, and then make the final deal public to give stakeholders an opportunity to decide whether they support it or not. This was crucial during the negotiations that led to the drafting of the US Constitution. The same approach—making an effort to minimize media coverage and leaks—was pursued in the negotiations that led to the peace agreement in Northern Ireland, and during CBA negotiations in the NFL and NHL. It is also why early-stage negotiations between governments and armed groups are usually kept secret until there is sufficient momentum to allow each side to admit that it has been negotiating. Peace processes are never announced on day one; there is almost always back-channel activity to help create the foundation for talks. The likelihood that talks will collapse is especially high at the start, making it risky for governments and insurgents to let their constituents know that they are attempting a diplomatic solution to the conflict. Only when there is evidence to suggest that both sides are interested in and capable of pursuing a negotiated agreement will either side incur the cost of announcing negotiations.

While it is easy to understand why stakeholders would demand complete transparency throughout the process, if you are trying to negotiate an end to protracted conflicts, this is unadvisable. Of course, the process should ensure that constituents ultimately decide whether a final agreement should be accepted. But negotiators should be given the space they need to structure the best agreement they can.

Transparency during the bargaining process can stifle progress. Give negotiators the privacy they need to structure the deal; give constituents the right to decide whether the deal is acceptable.

The principle of forward momentum is a reminder that one way to judge the wisdom of our tactics and process choices is from the point of view of their likely impact on our ability to make progress in the days, months, and years ahead. As we have seen, negotiators might sacrifice progress if they are too focused on solving short-term problems or achieving short-term gains. But progress in the *current* negotiation is not the only potential victim of short-termism. A myopic approach to negotiating, even if a deal is reached, can exacerbate the likelihood of future conflict, or diminish our ability to resolve it.

How our behavior today will affect our ability to negotiate future conflicts is a question that is too often ignored, perhaps because our limited resources (e.g., time, attention, leverage) tempt us to focus myopically on the demands of the current deal. But history demonstrates quite clearly—not just in sports, but in personal relationships, business, international relations, and elsewhere—that today's conflicts are often the result of how we conducted and concluded past negotiations. Effective negotiators keep this in mind. As the following chapter illustrates, even in seemingly intractable conflicts, it is important and possible to set a better course for future engagement.

10

STAY AT THE TABLE

Peacemaking from Vienna to Paris

THE FIRST WORLD WAR (1914–1919) has been labeled "the war to end all wars." In fact, it may have been better described as "the war that forgot all wars." Whether we look at the catastrophic decisions that led to the outbreak of war or at the structure of the flawed peace agreements that followed, we discover the tragic consequences of faded memories and of lessons too easily forgotten. Much has been said about the mistakes made in the Paris negotiations at the end of WWI, especially regarding how the treatment of defeated Germany likely played an important role in Germany's march towards instigating World War II. Of course, we sit in the privileged position of the future, making such judgments with the clarity of hindsight. Surely, if the victors had the ability to know better, they would have negotiated a different agreement. Alas, they did know better—and it did not help.

The hundred years of history prior to WWI were particularly notable for the relative absence of continental conflict in Europe. There were conflicts, to be sure, but none had escalated to the point of sustained multilateral wars with massive casualties. At least some of the credit for this goes to the negotiations that ended the previous great military conflict. The Napoleonic Wars had ended in 1814, and the victorious nations of Great Britain, Russia, Prussia, and Austria had come together in Vienna to decide the fate of defeated France.[1] In much the same way, 105 years later, Great Britain, France, Italy, and the United States came together in Paris to decide the fate of Germany. In each case, the defeated nation was seen as having been responsible for the destruction that had been caused by the war. In each case, most of the negotiations took place on one side of the table: the peace terms were largely decided by the victors and imposed on the defeated nation with little room for further bargaining. Yet, on at least one crucial dimension, the outcomes of these two negotiations could not have been more different.

How were the combatants in 1814 able to avoid the kinds of postwar turmoil that the peacemakers in 1919 seem to have encouraged? How do you stop a resurgence of the misdeeds and mistrust that have just led to a devastating war?

WITHOUT MONEY OR MUSCLE

The Congress of Vienna (and a treaty signed earlier that year in Paris) had forced France to give up the land it had conquered in recent years, but it was allowed to return to its expansive borders of 1789. While appropriately considered the aggressor, France was not initially asked to pay war reparations, lest this burden lead the country to become so weak that it would tempt belligerence in the form of either future French aggression or the conquest of a weakened France by other nations. This policy changed when Napoleon restarted the war, after escaping from exile in 1815. After the second defeat, France was forced to pay reparations, which it did in full.[2] Most importantly, in 1818, after France had made amends, it was invited to join the international community in what became known as the Concert of Europe. The multilateral conferences of the Concert of Europe were the closest thing to a United Nations or European Union that Europe would see until the next century.[3] Despite having been the perpetrators of war, the French were given a seat at the table.

In contrast, a century later at the end of World War I, the Allies did not treat Germany so astutely. Ironically, but not surprisingly, given the mistrust and animosity that had been growing since at least the Franco-German War of 1870, it was the French who spearheaded the attack on Germany during the peace negotiations.[4] When the smoke cleared, in addition to accepting severe restrictions on its military, Germany had to relinquish approximately 13% of its territory, 10% of its population, and all of its colonies outside of Europe.

The spirit of the deal can be best understood in two other key provisions. The first, Article 231 (AKA the "War Guilt Clause"), required the

Germans to "accept the responsibility of Germany and her allies for causing all the loss and damage." As such, Germany was expected to pay reparations to the tune of almost half a trillion dollars (in current dollars), a much higher amount than France had been required to pay in 1815, when measured as a percentage of GDP. But it was the second decision that was likely more consequential symbolically and substantively: disallowing Germany from joining the League of Nations, the precursor to the United Nations.

The German perspective on the take-it-or-be-invaded offer was perhaps best captured by Foreign Minister Brockdorff-Rantzau, who summarized the treaty as follows: "Germany surrenders all claims to its existence."[5]

CREATE A PROCESS FOR RESOLVING RESIDUAL CONFLICT

While there has been much debate over whether the Germans could have afforded to pay the reparations demanded of them—they quite possibly could have done so—the fact remains that these demands sowed the seeds for future conflict. However, as we can see in the case of France after the Napoleonic Wars, the imposition of even substantial reparations is not a *sufficient* condition for the outbreak of future conflict. Reparations and other punitive measures may increase the likelihood of conflict, but if there are structures and channels in place for peaceably managing residual or latent conflict, future wars may be avoidable. A potentially bigger mistake in dealing with Germany was not the reparations, but the isolation: the outcome fueled conflict *while simultaneously limiting the possibility of managing conflict.* Indeed, it is the isolation of the enemy, far more than a demand for reparations, that distinguishes the peace negotiations in Vienna from those in Paris.

Most influential delegates at the Congress of Vienna in 1814 shared a belief that it was imperative to be forward-looking. The statesmen in Vienna seemed to care more about preventing future wars than about punishing the perceived perpetrators of past wars. They acted to secure peace on behalf of future generations, not merely to exact vengeance on behalf of current victims. Most notably, by including France among the community of nations, and by creating a system in which the balance of power would not tip too strongly against the victors *or against the defeated,* the Europeans assured themselves a relatively long-lasting peace. It was not so in 1919.

Most negotiations, even successful ones, leave residual conflict in their wake. Create channels and processes to manage subsequent flare-ups and latent conflict.

STAY AT THE TABLE

The problem of underinvesting in continued engagement exists in all kinds of conflicts. When peace talks disintegrate, and especially if armed conflict flares up as a result, there is a tendency to break off all communication or negotiation rather than keep channels open to facilitate a future attempt at peacemaking. Then, even when future opportunities for deal making arise, there is a debilitating lack of information and understanding; the lack of investment in maintaining relationships makes subsequent agreements that much more difficult to achieve. In sports, at least historically, there has been a tendency among some negotiators to engage with each other only when a new collective bargaining agreement is on the horizon, rather than to build trust in the interim years. Similarly, the recent nuclear negotiations between the United States and Iran were hampered in no small part by the lack of relations over the previous decades. Some salespeople, too, will disengage with customers after a deal is signed (or when it fails), and reengage only when it is time to pitch the next deal.

A wiser strategy, in each instance, is to *stay at the table,* at least figuratively, if not physically, even when there is no visible prospect for a deal, or money to be made. Especially in the aftermath of "failed" negotiations, the natural tendency is for the relationship to further deteriorate, for trust to diminish, and for perspectives to diverge further. Continued engagement is crucial to keep relationships intact, audit the potentially changing interests and constraints of all parties, and explore the possibility of renewed negotiations. Also, it is often easier to obtain information and build trust when substantive negotiations are not under way, because there is less anxiety that sharing information will give the other side an advantage in a deal. My advice to deal makers is to stay engaged regardless of the outcome; there may come a time when the deal you reached can be improved, or the no deal you reached can be reversed.

Stay at the table, especially after failed negotiations, to sustain relationships, understand the other side's perspective, and look for opportunities to reengage.

IF YOU'RE NOT AT THE TABLE, YOU'RE ON THE MENU

In the case of WWI, it is not as if the potential problems with the peace deal were entirely unforeseen. Delegates from many countries openly worried that they had sown the seeds of future war. The notable exception was France, where some felt the terms were too lenient. A British officer at the time, Earl Wavell, described what occurred in 1919 with a touch of dark poetics: "After the 'war to end war' they seem to have been pretty successful in Paris at making the 'peace to end peace.'"[6] Why, despite such misgivings, did the treaty take the shape that it did?

One important reason was that the Germans were almost entirely excluded from the negotiations. In contrast, in 1814, the French had been given a seat at the table almost from the beginning, in no small part due to some brilliant maneuvering by the French diplomat (Talleyrand), although they had less of a voice than the other nations. In the absence of the German perspective in the room in 1919 (while the deal was being drafted), there was far too much momentum going against the Germans for far too long. There was simply no opposing force to balance the French demands. Not surprisingly, those with a seat at the negotiation table will sometimes ignore or even exploit the interests of those who are not represented. Indeed, a saying that has made the rounds in diplomatic and political circles gets right to the point: *If you're not at the table, you're on the menu.* In this case, the Germans were the appetizer, main course, and dessert.

The same holds true in all kinds of negotiations. Consider for example what typically happens in CBA negotiations in American sports. After months spent stubbornly resisting any calls for substantive concessions, the two sides eventually begin to move away from their opening positions. Which concessions do you think they make first? You do not need to know anything about sports, or even know which sport is being discussed, to be able to predict with great accuracy that one of the first big concessions that players will make is going to be related to rookie salaries and contracts. Why are the interests of rookies—the new players who are just entering the league—usually the first sacrifice made on the altar of collective bargaining? Because they are not at the table.

If you are not at the table, you are on the menu.

NEGOTIATING WITHOUT A SEAT AT THE TABLE

Wise negotiators do what they can to get a seat at the table. If that is not possible, there are other ways to influence what happens in a negotiation. In the 2011 NFL negotiations, for example, retired players did not have voting power in the negotiation, but they were able to influence the NFL Players Association and the league by using a sustained media campaign on retiree health concerns. More generally, if you have no formal role or leverage in the substantive negotiations, you may be able to influence those who do have control. Your leverage in these situations stems from your ability to help them from the outside. For example, they may have interests outside of the current deal that you can support in exchange for their support in the current negotiation. Or, they may need your help selling the current deal, as was the case with the retired players. If those at the table value your support or fear your opposition during the negotiation (or when it is time to ratify or sell the deal), you have leverage.

If you don't have a seat at the table, you might influence deal makers by creating value outside of the deal, or by offering to help sell or implement the current deal.

UNDERINVESTING IN PROCESS DURING TIMES OF PEACE

In his book *Diplomacy*, Henry Kissinger suggests a second reason why the peace negotiations in 1919 and 1814 took different shapes.[7] In 1814, the memory of past wars was vivid. For the previous few centuries, Europeans had not gone more than a few years without seeing war break out among great European powers. The prospect of continued and escalating conflicts was considered real, even assured, unless great effort was made to prevent it. In 1919, in contrast, the Great War (WWI) was seen as more of an accident or an anomaly, rather than the rule. It seemed to demand explanation *(How did it happen?)*, rather than effort *(How to prevent it in the future?)*. What the negotiators did not fully appreciate was that the long era of peace that ended with WWI had been the product of careful "system building," not an inevitable consequence of history's quest towards enlightenment.

This is an all too common problem in negotiated agreements in long-term relationships. When the context of a deal is forgotten and memories have faded, it becomes difficult for future generations of negotiators to understand the logic behind the original deal and why it might make sense to retain it. Instead, the deal begins to look flawed or inappropriate and no longer relevant. According to Dr. Kissinger, this explains why the British, after a few decades of peace following the Congress of Vienna, started to step away from their role as guarantors of the balance of power in Europe; it explains why the Austrians, within two generations of the Congress of Vienna, began to risk the system of alliances on which their survival depended to pursue short-term gains and temptations; it explains why the Germans, who had now consolidated power, traded away their treaty with the Russians to woo the British. In each case, statesmen failed to see that they had *purchased* peace by paying what, in the absence of war, seemed like unnecessary costs. For example, the British saw peace and felt their investment in Europe was unnecessary, rather than viewing the peace as a consequence of their investment. Likewise, the Austrians and Germans failed to appreciate that the freedoms they enjoyed were rooted in the alliances that they were now ready to squander.

Let's take this to a corporate context. Imagine a new CEO who walks into the office and finds that there have been no legal disputes in the last ten years and therefore decides that there is no longer any reason to invest in a legal team or in drafting contracts carefully with vendors and customers. Or, in sports, imagine a soccer team that discovers that the other team has not scored a single goal in the first half of the game and decides to pull the goalie for the second half. These decisions would be unthinkable. Unfortunately, in conflict environments, people will often make very similar decisions.

When "success" is not assessed in terms of a measurable "gain" but by the maintenance of a positive status quo (e.g., peace, continued cooperation, etc.), the causal link between effort and success may be unobservable. Without careful examination, it is not obvious what is keeping things on track. And if the policies designed to promote cooperation are costly—financially, politically, bureaucratically—there is a temptation to stop investing in them. Entropy ensues: in the absence of deliberate investment, relationships, institutions, and collaborative enterprises can all too easily deteriorate.

Companies seem to underinvest in strengthening stakeholder relationships when times are good, only to find they are short on goodwill when conflict arises. In the domain of armed conflict, the onset of insurgency is often preceded by political marginalization and procedural injustices perpetrated by a dominant group that seems to take the peaceful status quo for granted. In an entirely different context, the same principle might be useful in explaining why some in the United States have been caught up in the so-called anti-vaccination fad in recent years. Once a disease such as measles is largely eradicated and people do not have experience with the devastation it brings, it is easy to disparage the very vaccines that suppressed the disease and provided the comfort from which vaccine deniers wage their attacks. In each of these cases, the problem is not an unwillingness to invest in factors that sustain peace, nor is it the undervaluing of peace itself, but a failure to see how one leads to the other.

There is a tendency, especially in times of peace, to underinvest in processes that can help maintain relationships and in institutions that can help sustain the peace.

As with preparation, there is a wide disparity in how much negotiators focus on process. Some ignore it entirely; others strategize and negotiate process with incredible forethought. While we have seen the importance of negotiating process, this is not to say that you cannot overemphasize it. As the next chapter illustrates, there can be too much focus on process. When process takes on too much importance and becomes overladen with significance or symbolism, it can seriously damage prospects for substantive progress.

11

THE LIMITS OF PROCESS

Trying to End the Vietnam War

THE VIETNAM WAR (1955–1975) was ostensibly fought between North Vietnam and South Vietnam, but it is often regarded as having been a proxy war between the Soviet Union and the United States. The United States and its allies supported the South Vietnamese government based in Saigon. The Soviets, along with other communist states, supported the North Vietnamese and the National Liberation Front (NLF, AKA the Viet Cong), a heavily armed communist insurgency in the South. Although US involvement in Vietnam dates to the early 1950s, the watershed moment for increased US military involvement occurred in August 1964. This is when the infamous "Gulf of Tonkin" incidents took place. In two separate incidents, the US Navy reported attacks initiated by the North Vietnamese. These gave President Johnson the justification to ask Congress to authorize an expanded military campaign against the North.

Arguments still persist about whether legitimate US national interests were at stake in trying to keep Vietnam from "turning communist," but there is no debate about the reprehensible manner in which congressional support was garnered. As it turns out, in the first Tonkin incident, it was the United States that had initiated the attack, not the North Vietnamese. As for the second incident—it never occurred.[1] President Johnson and his administration were aware of the grave uncertainty surrounding the alleged attacks, but this was neither admitted, nor reported to Congress. The Gulf of Tonkin Resolution passed overwhelmingly and paved the way for what is now largely considered a disastrous escalation. More than 58,000 Americans died, and while estimates vary, so did well over a million others.

By 1968, it was evident that US military success was unlikely in Vietnam, especially given strong opposition to the war among the American public. The year started with the Tet Offensive, a massive urban military campaign in which the North Vietnamese Army and their NLF allies attacked scores of cities in the South. While the US and South Vietnamese response to the Tet Offensive was arguably a military success, it was achieved at tremendous cost: extensive casualties and large-scale disenchantment with the war effort. Perhaps unsurprisingly, 1968 was also the year that peace negotiations were initiated.

Peace would not be easy to achieve. One of the first stumbling blocks was a five-month delay, between May and October of 1968, during which the North Vietnamese refused to come to the negotiation table until President Johnson stopped bombing North Vietnam. Eventually, air strikes were halted, making way for the start of substantive negotiations—or so the would-be peacemakers might have hoped. Negotiating the conditions under which parties will come to the bargaining table is a common enough problem. But what to do when the parties are ready to come to the table, but cannot even agree on the shape of the table? On this issue, referred to obliquely in diplomatic cables as "the procedural matter," the parties reached an impasse.

AN UNHEALTHY OBSESSION WITH PROCESS

The problem surfaced in early December. The North Vietnamese (NV) wanted a square table at which the parties to the conflict would sit, each with its respective flag: North Vietnam, NLF, South Vietnam, and the United States of America. The South Vietnamese (SV) wanted two rectangular tables facing each other, one for each side of the conflict because, from their point of view, there were only two parties to the conflict, North and South. More importantly, the South was unwilling to accept the NLF as a legitimate party in the conflict. What followed can best be described as the most awesomely absurd investment of diplomatic ingenuity in history.[2]

On December 11, the ambassador from the SV delegation reiterated to the Americans his position that maintaining the "two-sides formula" was crucial and that no concession on this issue would be acceptable. A number of other shapes were then proposed by the Americans, with the argument that these were "not concessions but alternatives" that "were consistent with the two-sides principle: two semi-circles; four tables, two facing two; a diamond broken in two places; and a round table." The SV delegation held firm on what it considered to be its best offer: two long tables facing each other.

The following day, the American delegation sent a message to President Johnson informing him of an additional procedural challenge: the order of speaking. "It is agreed that names will be drawn at random from a hat; but [NV] wants four names drawn... to underline this is a 'four power' conference. We and the [SV] want only two names drawn, symbolizing our view that this is a 'your-side, my-side' conference. The two members of each side would then speak." Meanwhile, table-shape negotiations continued: the NV proposed using four separate tables, and then suggested a round table with all parties sitting around it, an idea that the US had previously failed to sell to the SV.

The delays continued, and not without risks: advice to President Johnson included the possibility of restarting air strikes "as a response to foot-dragging at the conference table." A member of the US delegation pointed out to the vice president of South Vietnam that "people in the US, and elsewhere in the world, and... even in Vietnam itself, could not be expected to understand our arguing over table shapes and who would speak in what order while the fighting and dying continued." But no solutions were forthcoming.

The SV vice president then proposed adopting a three-phased process, with the first phase focused only on issues that "had nothing to do with the NLF." This way, the NLF could be naturally excluded, without reliance on an agreement on table shape. The US would not support the proposal on the grounds that it was too transparent and would derail talks before they began. The Americans also started to consider the option of negotiating bilaterally with the North if the South was too rigid on matters of procedure.

On January 2, 1969, some progress was made. The North was still insisting on a "simple, round table" but had agreed to the SV position on having no flags or nameplates if the table-shape issue could be resolved. On speaking turns, the North agreed to the US proposal of two lots being drawn instead of four, but they insisted that the people doing the drawing be representatives of the SV and the NLF, not the US and NV. The SV were unimpressed with the concessions they had won and demanded that if a round table was to be used, it must have a cloth strip running down the middle of it to clearly signify two sides to the circle. The exasperated US team tried to argue that the clarity of two sides could be just as easily achieved by how closely different people sat to each other.

On January 4, the SV offered a way to resolve the issue of who would draw lots: they could "simply toss a coin, or let the other speak first." The US, meanwhile, considered whether the SV would be willing to settle the matter of an "unmarked" versus "divided" round table with a coin toss. The US also started to work on ensuring that the conference attendees enter the room from two separate entrances, thereby further highlighting the two-sided nature of the talks. US efforts throughout were aimed at quelling flabbergasted public opinion on this issue, as well as starting substantive talks before the new US President, Richard Nixon, came into office on January 20. The hope was that the SV could be convinced to agree to having an unmarked round table in exchange for NV concessions on flags, nameplates, and speaking turn.

For lack of a solution, the table-shape dispute was escalated to the head of state. On January 7, an exasperated President Johnson told his team, "I'm fed up!" and wondered aloud whether SV intransigence was somehow being fomented by the incoming Nixon administration. He then sent a letter to the SV president, in which he put the full force of the American presidency behind the demand for a simple, round conference table:

> Neither the American public nor the American Congress can understand our inability to accept a continuous, and if necessary unmarked, round table. Such a table is not inherently four-sided in any way. With space at the table divided, as it would be, on a 50–50 basis, the table would indeed have a clear two-sided tendency even if it were not marked. . . . At the present moment, the situation in the Congress and in the American public is as dangerous and volatile as I have seen it at any time in the last four years, or indeed in my 40 years of

> public service. Failure to make these reasonable adjustments in our position can only mean a real avalanche of criticism directed in part at the American Government, but far more acutely and damagingly at the image of your government in the American Congress and with the American people. . . . You and I have a long history of close and constructive collaboration. We have tried always to do the right thing, and this is what I am asking you to do now—in the firm belief that it is right, and in the equally firm belief that it is essential if my country is to go on with the basic course of action which I have supported throughout. Please do not force the United States to reconsider its basic position on Viet-Nam.[3]

Before handing the letter to the SV president, the US delegate reiterated the US position that the time had come to settle this issue.

> We will take measures to make clear that the table arrangement is essentially two-sided. This can be done in several ways. One way, which we had discussed earlier, involves leaving a space between our side and their side, by removing one chair at each mid-point or leaving it unoccupied. Another way is to put a pile of books or files of briefing papers on top of the table between our side and their side. . . . It is now more than two months since the final bombing halt, over a month since the GVN [Government of Vietnam] delegation arrived in Paris, eight months since the talks began in Paris between the United States and DRV, and in the view of my government the time has definitely come when we must move to substantive matters on which we can together present a firm united front. The issue of the shape of the table is a liability for both of us.[4]

And yet, the negotiations continued. There was even some debate about the difference between a round and a circular table. Eventually, the SV offered another compromise solution, in which the cloth strip could be replaced by a "thin but visible line separating the two sides." On the speaking issue, a new possibility arose: "drawing from two lots, e.g., one red and one yellow. The drawing to be by a third party (possibly a French official)."

Not for a lack of persistence or ingenuity up to this point, but it turns out that sometimes you just need a new set of eyes to see the problem.

With impasse looming, a new proposal was introduced on January 13 by the minister-counselor of the Soviet Embassy in France: "a round table with two small rectangular tables adjacent at opposite sides." Success was within reach!

On January 16, the disputing parties agreed to the following: A circular unmarked table with two rectangular tables at opposite points of the circle, 45 centimeters from it. There would be no flags or name plates. A French diplomat would draw lots or toss a coin to determine which side spoke first. The side that won would speak first with two speeches permitted. One final, albeit minor, problem did surface: the SV president did not want the coin flip to take place at the Quai, as initially proposed, but rather at the Hotel Majestic. This, mercifully, did not derail matters. The first meeting of the Paris peace talks began on the morning of January 18, 1969, at the Hotel Majestic.

When you have spent six weeks discussing the shape of a table, you can be sure that actual peace will not be easily achieved. The Paris Peace Accords were not signed until 1973, at which point a cease-fire was agreed to and the United States began its official withdrawal from the war. Although the *Agreement on Ending the War and Restoring Peace in Vietnam* called for a cease-fire, to be followed by a peaceful political process for resolving governance issues, the war in fact continued on until North Vietnam defeated the South and established a communist government in the entire country.

GETTING STUCK ON PROCESS: COMMON REASONS

As is evident here, it is certainly possible for negotiators to get bogged down with process concerns. For example, parties in a dispute might never get to the point where they discuss potential solutions if they can't decide who will make the initial settlement offer. A business deal that is expected to be good for both sides might still fail to materialize if one side wants a decision to be made quickly, but the other side prefers more time to shop around or to consider alternative options. In each case, the parties are understandably concerned about getting the process right, but getting stuck on process can lead to costly delays or put the possibility of reaching agreement in jeopardy.

There are a few common reasons why this happens. Sometimes it is due to *insufficient groundwork:* negotiators have not given enough thought to process issues, or differing views on the same team have not been reconciled in advance, complicating the discussions with the other side. Other times, it is *analysis-paralysis* that keeps parties from agreeing to a path forward: no process is "perfect," and the pursuit of an optimal process can lead to unnecessary delays. In some cases, it is an overblown *desire for strategic flexibility* (wanting to "keep all options open") that delays commitment on process, even though further delays are costly. All of these problems can be prevented, or at least mitigated, with adequate preparation.

Parties can get bogged down with process concerns when there is inadequate preparation, an unrealistic goal of crafting the perfect process, or an excessive desire for strategic flexibility.

WHEN TO LEAVE PROCESS BEHIND

As much as we might like to think of *substance* and *process* as being independent elements in deal making or diplomacy—each requiring a strategic approach—they often become intertwined in the minds of the negotiators and/or their audiences. To some degree, this is appropriate. Parties may recognize that decisions such as "who is in the room" and "how long will the negotiations last" can have substantive impact, and when this is true, these discussions should not be taken lightly. At the same time, an excessive focus on crafting the perfect or most advantageous process is a recipe for disaster. When this happens, the transition from process negotiation to substantive deal making is put in peril. In an ideal world, negotiators would set aside substantive discussions until there is a viable process in place. However, when it seems that prolonged process discussions are putting at risk the possibility of progress on substance, it may be wiser to (a) try to reach agreement on an imperfect process that can be revised later, or (b) start substantive negotiations in parallel with ongoing process negotiations.

If substantive discussions are being thwarted by an excessive focus on process, (a) consider reaching an agreement on an imperfect but revisable process, or (b) begin substantive discussions in parallel with process discussions.

PROCESS CONFLICT AS A PROXY WAR FOR LEGITIMACY AND LEVERAGE

The problem is greater when the parties see even minor concessions on process as tantamount to sacrificing significant leverage or legitimacy in the deal. This is especially likely when there is uncertainty or ambiguity surrounding who has the dominant position. It is easier to settle on a process when the status-hierarchy and power dynamics are well established and stable, because neither side perceives much benefit in jockeying for position in the early stages of engagement. But when there is no mutually acknowledged pattern of deference, process *becomes* substance. As strange as it may seem to outside observers, to those embroiled in such conflicts even seemingly trivial issues surrounding the rules of engagement are seen as the earliest tests of resolve, leverage, and legitimacy. We see this clearly in a pointed dispatch from the American Embassy to the US State Department, on December 19, which included the following assessment of the table-shape negotiations:

> . . . the [SV] made some points which in their view go to the very heart of the problem, especially that they must not be placed on the same footing as the National Liberation Front. The [SV] regards these matters as of the utmost importance. They see the initial moves as critical, believing the enemy will conclude from them whether he can get us to make important concessions on matters of substance and whether he can divide the US and the [SV]. . . . To the North Vietnamese—as to the South Vietnamese, procedure is substance, because procedure can determine substance. The South Vietnamese fear that we

> may be over eager to make concessions . . . I think they are right in their assessment of the effect of premature concessions on the climate here in South Viet-Nam. If our side caves in during the first preliminary round, there could be a serious decline in morale here. People will judge the chances of freedom in South Viet-Nam, and the firmness of our commitment to that freedom, by how we handle ourselves—the US and the [SV] together—during the opening phase of the talks. The enemy said for years he would not negotiate while the bombing went on, then he did negotiate while the bombing went on, said we had to meet in Phnom Penh or Warsaw, and then he agreed to meet in Paris. He said he would not accept conditions in return for the bombing halt; finally he did accept conditions.... He now says that he will not sit down unless the "four-sided" character of the negotiations is recognized. Since we are not going to recognize that, he will settle for less. With the Communists (indeed, in my experience, this is not confined to the Communists), fruitful negotiations are rarely advanced by being accommodating, especially at the beginning. In fact, I believe that by showing ourselves too eager for early results, we may make the achievement of a viable solution to the conflict more difficult and more time consuming in the end.[5]

When power relations are unclear or unstable, process negotiations can become proxy wars for leverage and legitimacy, endangering substantive negotiations.

THE CASE FOR TAKING A STAND ON PROCEDURAL ISSUES

This is not to say that taking a tough stand on process is never a good idea. In fact, how you behave during process negotiations can have an effect on how the other side will treat you in substantive negotiations. Not long ago, I was advising a small company that was negotiating a strategic partnership with a much larger company that had many billions of dollars in annual revenue. There was goodwill on both sides of the table, but it became apparent early on that the other team was planning on treating us like all other small companies with whom they had dealt—which is to say, they would dictate terms and expect us to nod along. To be fair, there was no real ill intent. From their perspective, there were plenty of small firms lining up for a chance to associate with them because they offered tremendous brand value and huge distribution capability. The problem was that we did not see ourselves as a struggling start-up. To the contrary, an objective assessment would reveal that we also brought tremendous value to them, specifically addressing one of their major strategic needs.

From my perspective, the problem was about the psychology of the deal: *they knew and we knew* that we brought at least as much value as they did, but *they assumed we would acknowledge* that this would not be a discussion among equals. I told our team that we needed to keep in mind that the other party negotiated deals with two kinds of partners: those they considered equals and those they thought should feel lucky to even be there. Because they treated these two groups very differently, we needed to make sure that the "equals" frame, not the "lucky" frame, was established from the outset. If the "lucky" frame took hold, we would be expected to defer throughout the deal-making process.

So I advised that we make a stand early on, and to make it on process. More specifically, we decided we would push back on even very small process demands if we believed these would not have been imposed on someone who was considered an equal. In the early weeks, there was more back-and-forth on process than either side would have liked, but it did the trick. By the time we got to substantive negotiations, it was much easier for us—and not at all surprising to them—when we stood firm against anything that seemed asymmetric or unfair.

Resisting unfair demands on matters of substance is easier if you have earlier challenged unfair demands on process.

HOW TO STAND FIRM ON PROCESS

Why did our approach to negotiating with the large firm not devolve into the kind of nonsense witnessed in Vietnam? Obviously, there are countless differences between the two situations, but here are a few things to keep in mind when deciding to put your foot down on process. First, we were motivated by a desire for equal footing, not vying for advantage over the other side. Conflicts are much more likely to spiral out of control if you are perceived as trying to achieve a dominant position. We sent a consistent message regarding this motivation because we not only pushed back on *their* one-sided demands but also avoided language or proposals that could be interpreted as wildly asymmetric in our favor. Second, we understood that process and substance are sometimes linked, and we were careful not to let process disputes interfere with substantive considerations. For example, a discussion regarding deadlines (process) can have an impact on the scope of the deal you will be able to negotiate (substance). Likewise, whether you agree to an exclusive negotiating period has both process and substantive consequences. In such cases, look for ways to separate process and substantive concerns. For example, to meet one side's deadline for announcing the deal and the other side's interest in a broader scope for the partnership, you can structure the deal so that it takes full shape in phases. To reconcile the other side's desire for your complete attention during the deal-making phase with your interest in maintaining leverage, you could agree to partial or provisional exclusivity, to be extended on the basis of progress. Finally, we negotiated process in parallel with substance. Unlike what happened in Vietnam, the negotiators at the Vietnam peace talks did not let the lack of a fully articulated process delay progress on substantive issues when progress on substance seemed possible and beneficial.

If you want to stand firm on process, it is best to (a) demonstrate that you seek equality, not advantage, (b) acknowledge and address substantive concerns that are linked to process choices, and (c) negotiate substance in parallel with process.

Throughout this section we have seen how negotiating the process—without letting it get out of hand—can help avoid or overcome deadlock and conflict. In the final chapter of this section, let's zoom out and think about how effective negotiators can act with foresight to entirely reshape the terms of future engagement.

12

CHANGING THE RULES OF ENGAGEMENT

Negotiating with Your Friends

IN FEBRUARY 2002, NBC and Warner Brothers made headlines when they signed the most expensive deal in television history for the rights to a 30-minute sitcom. The show was *Friends,* a situation comedy about six friends living in New York City. This would be the tenth and final season, ending a decade-long run in which the show was nominated for over 60 Primetime Emmy Awards (winning six) and was ranked in the top five shows on TV in all but its first season. It was undoubtedly a great show, but that is not enough to explain how much the actors playing the six main characters were paid for the final season.

Many comedies have one clear star surrounded by an ensemble of other characters. Consider, for example, some of the most popular shows on NBC in the two decades leading up to this negotiation: *The Cosby Show, Family Ties, Frasier, Everybody Loves Raymond,* and *Seinfeld.* What made *Friends* unique was that there were six characters, all of whom were given close to the same amount of screen time.[1] This made them all equally important. It could also make them, from a negotiation perspective, equally expendable. From the point of view of the production company or a TV network, if one cast member were to get too aggressive in bargaining, the show would likely be able to continue without him or her. It would not be an ideal situation, but having the ability to move forward with five of six original cast members should have provided some degree of leverage against the actors. (This kind of leverage is hard to muster when the show is called *Seinfeld* or *Everybody Loves Raymond,* and the actor's name happens to be Jerry Seinfeld or Raymond Romano.)

Yet, when all was said and done, the deal reached between NBC and Warner Brothers gave each of the six actors $1 million *per episode*. With 22 shows scheduled for the season, the actors would each stand to make $22 million.[2] To put this in perspective, consider the following: Only a few years earlier, in the final season for *Seinfeld*, a show that won more Emmys and did better in the ratings than *Friends*, Jerry Seinfeld was paid $1 million per episode; the next-highest-paid three actors were given $600,000 per episode.[3] How then were all six "friends" able to hold out for so much more?

WITHOUT MONEY OR MUSCLE

The seeds for success in 2002 were sown years earlier, during the negotiations for the third season of *Friends*. Prior to the third season, the six actors had always negotiated in the standard way, which is to say they negotiated separately with the help of their agents. After the first year, for which each actor was given a standard $22,500 per episode, their future salaries would be a function of the success of the show, the perceived importance of the character, and the outside options the actor had. In the second season, these factors resulted in a range of salaries for the six, between approximately $20,000 and $40,000 per episode.[4]

Before negotiations for the third season began, however, actor David Schwimmer ("Ross"), who was likely to make one of the highest salaries that season, came up with a different approach. He went to his fellow cast members and made the argument that the production company and TV network had tremendous leverage over them because, individually, each of them was replaceable. They would not be in a position to really share in the show's success unless they agreed to stick together in future negotiations and to ask for the same salary for each actor. This was unorthodox; Schwimmer was asking them to pay no attention to their individual value-add to the show and to instead negotiate based on their collective contribution. If they could somehow stick together regardless of who "objectively" deserved more or less in any given season, they would have increased leverage. Then he played his trump card. To underscore his own commitment to the idea, he offered to make the first sacrifice; he would ask the production company to *pay him less money* in the third season so that all of them would make the same amount. Jennifer Aniston ("Rachel") would have to agree to do the same—and she did. As a result, in that contract, each of them was paid the salary of the lowest-paid actor: starting at $75,000 per episode for Season 3, and increasing to $125,000 for Season 6.[5] They would never negotiate separately again.

David Schwimmer recalled, during an interview with *Vanity Fair*:

> I said to the group, "Here's the deal. I'm being advised to ask for more money, but I think, instead of that, we should all go in together. There's this expectation that I'm going in to ask for a pay raise. I think we should use this opportunity to talk openly about the six of us being paid the same. I don't want to come to work feeling that there's going to be any kind of resentment from anyone else in the cast down the line. I don't want to be in their position"—I said the name of the lowest-paid actor on the show—"coming to work, doing the same amount of work, and feeling like someone else is getting paid twice as much. That's ridiculous. Let's just make the decision now. We're all going to be paid the same, for the same amount of work." I thought it was significant for us to become a mini-union. Because there began to be a lot of decisions that had to be made by the group in terms of publicity. That was actually a by-product of how the impulse originated, which was from my ensemble theater [experience]. We all paid dues. We were all waiting tables and doing other jobs, but we all paid the same amount of dues, and we were all paid out equally. That idea was really important to me.[6]

In addition to higher salaries, the cast members were able to negotiate a share of syndication royalties—uncommon for an ensemble at the time—giving them a percentage of revenues once the show was in reruns. After the sixth season, the cast negotiated a salary of $750,000 per episode for each actor.[7] By the time the famed $1-million-per-episode negotiation took place, there was no doubt in anyone's mind that the six actors were going to either all sign or all walk away. Schwimmer's gambit—the sacrifice he made when tens of thousands of dollars were on the table—paid off in the millions.

SHAPE THE TERMS OF FUTURE ENGAGEMENT WHEN IT'S STILL CHEAP TO DO SO

Even the most important relationships usually begin with interactions that have relatively lower stakes. Wars often begin with skirmishes. Peace processes often start with attempts at a cease-fire. The possibility of an acquisition is often tested with joint activity in a more limited arena. The seeds of marriage are often planted in the first date. Some of the most successful business partnerships have begun with a few friends or colleagues sitting around chatting about an interesting idea.

Much has been said about the impact of first impressions, and there is no shortage of anecdotes and parables extolling the virtues of treating people well—even strangers—because you never know what comes out of it. The lesson here is a bit different: it is not merely about making a positive impression early in the relationship, but about *shaping the terms of engagement* early in the relationship. Schwimmer comes across as a very nice guy, and I'm sure that did not hurt. But what he suggested had less to do with his demeanor or likability: the substance of his proposal was that by investing today, the six actors had an opportunity to reshape the process of negotiation in a way that could be better for all of them in the long run.

Early-stage interactions can provide a relatively low-cost opportunity to shape the terms of future engagement.

COSTLY INVESTMENTS SIGNAL COMMITMENT TO PROCESS

It is one thing to come up with a good idea for how to reshape the process. It is another thing entirely to do so in a way that underscores your own commitment to the proposal. Notably, Schwimmer's proposal was not going to be costless; occasionally, one or more of the actors might be worse off with this arrangement. To articulate with credibility that he believed such costs were worth incurring, he took the first hit. The willingness to incur a cost early on when there is no guarantee that the investment will pay off is a powerful means of signaling commitment to a new way forward.

Governments or armed groups that incur political costs or accept preconditions for initiating a peace process send such a signal. Potential deal makers who agree to a hefty "break-up fee" if the deal does not happen, or to an exclusive negotiating period that may delay or eliminate other options, are also signaling commitment early on. Employees who agree to accept a job offer before negotiating the precise terms are doing the same. I know a CEO of an early-stage company that was struggling and in dire need of additional capital. There was tremendous anxiety among employees regarding what would happen if the company failed to ink another round of investment in the next few months. This created an incentive for them to start looking for other jobs right away, as a job search can take months as well. The CEO went to his key employees and asked them to delay any such plans. He told them that he was committed to the company and to them and that he needed them to also stay committed for a few more months before deciding to look elsewhere. And then he underscored his commitment by promising to pay their salaries from his own pocket if necessary (i.e., if the investors did not sign) to ensure that they would not start jumping ship at this moment of crisis.

Each of these types of decisions may be a bad one in some circumstances, and I do not recommend any of them with regularity. That is precisely the point: because these are risky, they can send a strong signal of commitment.

Your willingness to incur up-front costs in support of the process sends a credible signal of your commitment to it.

LABEL YOUR CONCESSIONS

Signaling that you are committed to the process does not do you much good if it does not encourage others to be committed as well. There is a danger here. When a government agrees to preconditions, it might end up signaling desperation rather than commitment to a worthy cause.

When an acquirer agrees to a large break-up fee, it may signal weakness rather than genuine interest. When an employee agrees to a job before negotiating, or a deal maker agrees to a lengthy exclusivity period, this may signal incompetence or a lack of alternatives rather than a positive commitment to the opportunity. Almost every behavior in negotiations can be interpreted in multiple ways. The very same act of goodwill—making a concession for the greater good—can be interpreted as *nice, smart, desperate,* or *stupid.*

Research shows that for best results—to make it most likely that the other side will reciprocate your actions with their own helpful acts—you want the other side to interpret your actions as being nice *and* smart.[8] Unfortunately, especially in difficult negotiations and ugly conflicts, the other side has every motivation to see your actions as being driven by nefarious intentions, desperation, irrationality, or incompetence. Wise negotiators try to manage the attributions others will make regarding their concessions. For example, before agreeing to a lengthy exclusivity period, the deal maker may want to mention or hint at her other alternatives (to avoid seeming desperate) and explain that, in this case, a lengthy exclusivity period is acceptable because "we understand the unique risks you face in entering into discussions at this time," thereby signaling empathy and competence. To put it simply, it is not enough that you make concessions that facilitate progress towards a mutually beneficial agreement; you often have to take it upon yourself to *label your concessions.* That is, make sure the other side is understanding the rationale for your actions, rather than jumping to conclusions. In the situationally appropriate way, you want to convey the message that what you did was a *choice,* that it was *costly,* and that you did it because you believe both sides understand the benefits of *mutual* cooperation.

In the case of *Friends,* the right attributions seem to have been made of Schwimmer's behavior. His co-star and friend, Matt LeBlanc ("Joey"), would later reflect:

> Schwimmer was in the position to make the most money. He was the A-story—Ross and Rachel. He could have commanded alone more than anyone else. . . . Did he know ultimately there would be more value in that for all of us as a

whole? I don't know. I think it was a genuine gesture from him, and I always say that. It was him.[9]

Label your concessions. Even genuine acts of kindness and wisdom can be interpreted as weakness or incompetence. Shape the attributions others will make of your behavior to ensure that you encourage reciprocity rather than exploitation.

IF A DESTRUCTIVE PATTERN IS ENTRENCHED, LABEL YOUR FUTURE CONCESSIONS

Earlier in the book, we discussed the importance of reframing quickly if a disadvantageous frame is in place. Of course, the sooner you challenge a disadvantageous frame, the sooner you are able to achieve your preferred outcome. But there is another reason to act quickly. The longer a frame persists and goes unchallenged, the harder it will be to change it later. For example, in labor–management relationships, if a contentious frame has been in place for decades and the owners call for a lockout each time they negotiate (e.g., in the NHL), it will be hard to change the pattern. Even if all sides want to improve the relationship, it will not be easy for owners to decide *against* issuing a lockout. If you've negotiated aggressively the last five times you came to the table, your well-intentioned decision to negotiate more amicably this time might actually be perceived as a sign of desperation. The longer you've been fighting, the harder it is to stop fighting without looking weak. Similar patterns often take hold in politics, and, sadly, too often in personal relationships as well; each time one side softens its stance, the other side is conditioned to take advantage of the opportunity.

One solution is to label your concessions; let the other side know that you are acting out of concern for the long-term relationship, not out of weakness. But if a pattern of fighting is entrenched, or if the frame of "eat-or-be-eaten" has persisted for too long, your labels may not be immediately credible. You may not be able to convince your negotiating partners in the heat of battle that you are actually "strong *and* nice" because they have never before seen you exhibit both of these traits at the same time.

From *their* point of view, you've only ever acted "nice" when you were in a position of weakness.

In such situations, it is sometimes more effective to *label your future concessions.* For example, you fight more aggressively than you had wanted to *today* because the alternative is to be seen as weak, but you propose a path that can lead to *future* cooperation by letting the other side know you are willing to behave differently next time *if* they will work with you to create the right conditions. These conditions could be an agreement that both sides will start out with less aggressive positions, that the media will not be used to attack each other, that concessions will be reciprocated in a timely manner, or that each side will just do its best not to respond to kindness with mistrust or aggression. Simply put, a concession today might not be possible to label, but a concession you have not yet made can be easier to label.

If a destructive pattern is entrenched, label your future concessions.

SAFEGUARD YOUR CREDIBILITY—AT TIMES IT WILL BE YOUR ONLY SOURCE OF LEVERAGE

As we've just discussed, not all negotiations provide an easy way to label your concessions and show your commitment to a process that would work better for everyone. You may not have the option, like David Schwimmer did, of incurring the first cost, and the people whom you have to convince of your motives may not trust you as much as the "friends" trusted him. But in my experience, there is one way to signal your commitment to process that *all* negotiations provide: *Always keep your word, even when it is costly.* The best deal makers and diplomats take very seriously the promises and commitments they have made to the other side on small things and big. This is not only the right thing to do; it is a tremendously powerful instrument in deal making. Especially in difficult, protracted conflicts where negotiating itself might be seen as risky or useless, often the only source of leverage you have for bringing the other side to the table is your credibility. And once you're at the table, mistrust is often the biggest barrier to the give-and-take necessary for progress, because many of the concessions either side commits to are not deliverable right away—promises of equitable treatment, power sharing, future benefits, etc. are necessarily premised on trust. If you have not built up a reputation for credibility, you are ill-suited to negotiate such deals.

Interestingly, in both big deals and small, people don't usually lose their credibility because of one sudden act of extreme treachery. Rather, credibility erodes slowly over time, as the other party starts to learn that we do not always follow through on our commitments; that we sometimes make strong assertions based on incomplete information; and that we seem to forget some of the assurances we gave, perhaps too hastily, in earlier discussions. As a consequence, the reason someone doesn't believe you when you honestly tell them "I cannot do that" is because some weeks or months ago you used the same language, only to do that very thing once it suddenly became worthwhile. I remind my students and clients often: *There will come a time when your only source of leverage in the negotiation will be your credibility.* It is unfortunate that this invaluable asset is so often traded away for so little, so casually.

Credibility is usually lost a little at a time. Safeguard your credibility by following through on your commitments, even the small ones.

SUMMARY OF LESSONS FROM PART II: THE POWER OF PROCESS

- Have a process strategy.
- Don't just strategize the negotiation process; strategize the implementation process.
- Be the most prepared person in the room.
- Negotiate process before substance.
- Synchronize with the other side on process.
- Seek clarity and commitment on process.
- Normalize the process and encourage others to normalize it for you.

- Even the other side's refusal to clarify or commit to process is informative.
- Seek commitments that are explicit, unambiguous, public, and personal.
- Before walking away because of a process breach, assess the other side's perspective, evaluate all consequences, and suggest viable remedies.
- Commitment to a very rigid process is not always possible or advisable.
- Preserve forward momentum. How will pursuing near-term advantage affect future engagement?
- Consensus has merits, but it gives everyone veto power and reduces the likelihood of agreement.
- Sufficient consensus helps preserve momentum and limits hostage-taking on individual issues.
- Keep a low bar for progress on individual issues, but a high bar for approving the final agreement.
- "Nothing is agreed until everything is agreed."
- Transparency can stifle progress. Allow for closed-door negotiations; then give constituents a say on the final deal.
- Even after successful negotiations, create channels and processes to manage residual and latent conflict.
- Stay at the table, especially after failed negotiations.
- If you are not at the table, you are on the menu.
- Get leverage when you are not at the table by helping sell the deal or by creating value elsewhere.
- Beware the tendency, during times of peace, to underinvest in the maintenance of peace.
- We get stuck on process because of inadequate preparation, wanting a perfect process, or wanting too much flexibility.
- To get unstuck, agree to a process that can be revised, or start negotiating substance in parallel with process.
- Process negotiations can become proxy wars for leverage and legitimacy.
- Resisting unfair demands on substance is easier if you earlier pushed back on unfairness in process.

- When standing firm on principle, seek equality, not advantage, and address any substantive concerns that are affected by your stance.
- Be the first mover in establishing the right process: shape the terms of future engagement.
- Your willingness to incur costs in support of the process sends a credible signal of your commitment.
- Label your concessions.
- If a destructive pattern is entrenched, label your future concessions.
- Safeguard your credibility by following through on your commitments, even the small ones.

Part III
THE POWER OF EMPATHY

Understanding, I think, is the most important thing when you are dealing with people—any people. You have got to make the effort to understand even the un-understandable.

LAKHDAR BRAHIMI

13
THE POWER OF EMPATHY

Negotiating the Cuban Missile Crisis

ON OCTOBER 16, 1962, American U-2 spy planes conducting reconnaissance over Cuba discovered what was later confirmed to be the construction, with help from the Soviet Union, of missile sites capable of launching nuclear weapons. The mere existence of missile sites in nearby Cuba was neither unexpected nor problematic, but two specific features of these sites were of particular concern to the United States. First, they would be capable of launching offensive missiles that could target the US mainland.[1] Second, the missiles were capable of carrying nuclear warheads. As it happens, the Soviet Union had promised publicly and privately that offensive missiles capable of carrying nuclear weapons would not be stationed in Cuba. It was now clear that these assurances had served only to deceive and to delay discovery of the missile sites. This set off what in the United States would come to be known as the Cuban Missile Crisis.[2]

As the conflict escalated, the world started to inch closer to a nuclear war than it has at any other time in history. On October 18, US President John F. Kennedy (JFK) organized a group of advisers, later dubbed the ExComm (Executive Committee of the President of the United States), that would convene secretly to assess options for how to respond to the threat. This group of more than a dozen people included the Joint Chiefs of Staff, the secretaries of defense and state, the national security advisor, the CIA director, and Robert Kennedy, who was both attorney general and JFK's younger brother.

Early on it became clear that there were two primary options for a US response. The first, which we might call the *aggressive* option, would entail immediate air strikes to take out the nascent missile sites, possibly followed by a land invasion of Cuba. The second option, which we might refer to as the *gradual* option, called for the imposition of a blockade to keep additional military equipment from reaching Cuba, followed by diplomacy and coalition building in South America and the United Nations; in this option, military strikes would be the measure of last resort. There were reasonable arguments on both sides, and both options were risky. The discussion among ExComm members revealed that there was not even agreement about which option would be more likely to lead to further escalation by the Soviet Union.

At the start of ExComm deliberations, almost everyone supported the aggressive option. Robert Kennedy was in the small minority who considered this to be too risky a strategy because it immediately limited options for both sides. He also felt that there was a strong moral argument to be made against a superpower unilaterally and preemptively attacking a small country. In the days that followed, the tide shifted, and the majority of the ExComm came to the conclusion that the gradual option was superior. From a historical perspective, almost everyone agrees that the shift from aggressive to gradual was wise. The reason is that we have learned a lot since 1962 about what was happening at the time in the Soviet Union and Cuba, and almost *every* piece of new information suggests that an aggressive (air-strikes/invasion) strategy would have been even more disastrous than the ExComm had imagined. In other words, every incorrect assumption the ExComm made was wrong in the same direction: it underestimated the risk of escalation in the event of a military strike. For example, the ExComm assumed there were roughly 10,000 Soviet troops in Cuba at the time; in fact, there were over 40,000. Consider how this increases the likelihood that the United States ends up killing so many Soviet troops that the Soviet Union feels it must retaliate. Also, the ExComm believed that although there were missiles in Cuba, the nuclear warheads were yet to be delivered. In fact, the nukes were already in Cuba, and the arsenal even included "tactical" nuclear weapons, the kind one might use on an invasion force. Finally, the ExComm took it as an article of faith that no Soviet nuclear weapon could be launched without explicit authorization from Soviet Premier Nikita Khrushchev. In fact, Soviet commanders in Cuba had the authority to use nuclear weapons at their discretion, and Cuban leader Fidel Castro had decided that nuclear weapons should be used if there were an invasion. US Secretary of Defense Robert McNamara, who had been part of the ExComm, would later explain the implications of this: "No one should believe that had United States troops been attacked with tactical nuclear warheads, the United States would have refrained from responding with nuclear warheads. And where would it have ended? In utter disaster."[3]

Disaster may have been avoided, at the outset, by moving to the gradual option, but choosing diplomacy is never a panacea. Just because the military option is terrible and you have opted to negotiate does not mean you will be able to reach an agreement—especially when you are negotiating in the shadow of time pressure, uncertainty, mutual mistrust, and deep-seated antagonism. How do you approach a negotiation in which no one is willing or able to back down, and when each delay and every misstep takes you closer to the brink of nuclear war?

NEGOTIATING THE IMPOSSIBLE

Instead of a preemptive military attack, the United States set up a naval blockade of Cuba, which they termed "quarantine" for political and strategic reasons. Then, in concert with a growing group of allies, and the threat of military escalation, the United States began to pressure the Soviet Union to negotiate an end to the crisis. An outcome acceptable to the Americans would require the Soviet Union to dismantle the missile sites and remove the missiles from Cuba. How could the United States convince the Soviets to do so, especially when *they* had shown a willingness to take grave risks for military advantage, while the United States had so far shown an unwillingness to escalate matters or flex too much muscle?

The key to resolving the crisis was not just a different approach from what had initially been favored, but an entirely different *perspective* on how the conflict should be viewed. What made the difference was JFK's willingness to consider *Khrushchev's* point of view, and to investigate precisely why the Soviet Union felt compelled to transfer nuclear weapons to

Cuba even when it risked starting a war. There were, it turns out, a number of such reasons—and understanding them was pivotal.

Consider the Soviet perspective. First, the United States already had nuclear-capable missiles stationed close to the Soviet Union, in Turkey and Italy, which were as threatening to the Soviets as the missiles in Cuba would be to the United States. Second, there was a significant "missile gap" at the time, with US nuclear capabilities (i.e., the number of missiles, bombers, and warheads) being an order of magnitude greater than those of the Soviet Union.[4] The US arsenal was also more technologically advanced. Third, the biggest problem with the Soviet arsenal was a scarcity of intercontinental ballistic missiles capable of reaching the United States in the event of war. The Soviets knew this problem could be overcome in a few years, but in the meantime, they believed a nuclear deterrent in the form of shorter range missiles stationed closer to the United States was badly needed. Finally, there was the issue of how the CIA kept hatching plans to assassinate or overthrow Fidel Castro, something the Soviet Union and Cuba found more than a little irksome.

Understanding this perspective went a long way in helping to end the crisis, but even then the path ahead was not easy. In the days that followed, as public and private diplomacy took shape, there were multiple crises and numerous decisions made under tremendous uncertainty. On one occasion, the US military deployed depth charges to force a Soviet submarine to surface, unaware that it was a *nuclear* submarine and that they had almost triggered a protocol that would cause it to launch its weapons. At another point during the crisis, Fidel Castro reached a moment of such despair that he sent Khrushchev a letter proposing a preemptive nuclear strike against the United States. Khrushchev, wisely, ignored the advice.

Ultimately, despite the important (but limited) use of military assets, and even after the missile sites became operational, it was not a military response but a negotiated agreement that resolved the conflict. The key elements of the deal were as follows. The Soviet Union would remove the missile sites under UN monitoring—which they did the following month. In exchange, the United States would end the quarantine and make two promises. First, the United States would deliver a "no-invasion" pledge regarding Cuba. Second, and crucially, the United States would dismantle the missiles based in Turkey and Italy that the Soviets considered threatening. But there was a twist. Fearing that this last concession would make the United States look weak, the Americans demanded that the removal of US missiles be a *secret* element of the deal; Khrushchev was told that if he publicized the American concession on missiles, the United States would no longer be able to follow through on it. In other words, Khrushchev could get a good deal, but he would not be able to declare victory. The possibility of a nuclear confrontation in the event of impasse may have tipped the scale in favor of doing the deal; Khrushchev agreed.

The US missiles were removed the following year, but Khrushchev lost his job soon after, at least in part because of the perception that the United States had "won" the standoff. Only decades later would the United States acknowledge publicly that JFK had, in fact, made a quid pro quo offer to remove US missiles in exchange for the removal of Soviet missiles.

EMPATHY CREATES MORE OPTIONS—FOR YOU

A successful end to this crisis would be unimaginable if not for President Kennedy's ability and willingness to consider the conflict from Khrushchev's point of view.[5] From the US perspective at the time, it would have been easy to see the Soviet Union as nothing more than an immoral state that was acting in an irresponsible and provocative manner, under the cover of lies and misdirection, to gain military advantage.

But the more important consideration from a negotiation perspective is always this: *How does the other side see their own behavior?* In fact, there would have been little appetite to even attempt diplomacy if JFK had not made an effort to consider the reasons why the Soviet Union would find its own actions justified. And once negotiations were under way, a solution was possible only because the United States understood the real motivations and concerns of the Soviet Union. This is the power and promise of empathy.

The mistake people make is to think that empathy is what you use when you want to be nice, or that it is an instrument of the weak. This reflects a dangerous flaw in understanding. For negotiators, the reason to empathize with the enemy is not because it is somehow the "nice" or "liberal" or "enlightened" approach to dealing with nasty people. We need to empathize because *it makes it more likely that we can achieve our own goals.* In the case of the Cuban Missile Crisis, for example, the negotiated solution would not have been possible—or imaginable—if President Kennedy had not empathized with Premier Khrushchev. Unless Kennedy acknowledged that the Russians might legitimately feel threatened by the US missiles in Turkey and Italy, the removal of these missiles, which was pivotal in resolving the conflict, would not even have been a concession worth considering. Why bother making such a concession if the real reason the other side is behaving this way is that it is evil or irrational?

In negotiations of all kinds, the greater your capacity for empathy—the more carefully you try to understand all of the other party's motivations, interests, and constraints—the more options you tend to have for potentially resolving the dispute or deadlock. In other words, when you empathize, you are not doing others a favor, you are doing yourself a favor. If the employer who refuses our request for a raise is immediately written off as callous, if the business partner who makes aggressive demands is too readily seen as greedy, if the political opposition is too quickly labeled evil or ill-intentioned, we limit our own options. Your boss may have real constraints. The business partner may genuinely believe her requests are reasonable. Your political opponents almost certainly believe that *they* are the ones doing what is best for the country. When we fail to explore their perspectives, we are unlikely to de-escalate conflict, find common ground, help each other address core concerns, or think creatively about how each side's interests might be met. *Empathy expands the set of options you have* for resolving conflict and reaching agreement. Empathy does not guarantee success, but a lack of empathy usually guarantees failure.

Empathy expands the set of options you have for resolving the conflict. The better you understand the other side's perspective, the more likely you are to find a solution.

EMPATHY IS NEEDED MOST WITH THOSE WHO SEEM TO DESERVE IT LEAST

Most of us see ourselves as being relatively understanding and empathetic, but we fail to act this way when we are dealing with people who have done things that we find abhorrent or inexplicable. Yet, these are precisely the situations where empathy is most needed. You already understand your friends; the key to resolving conflicts lies in understanding your enemies.

It is important not to confuse empathy with sympathy. The goal is to *understand* what is causing someone to behave a certain way; it does not mean you have to *approve* of their goals or actions. There is a difference between *explaining* the other side's behavior and *justifying* it. If we are to engage with them in any manner other than all-out war, and perhaps even then, we must seek to understand why *they* believe their actions are appropriate, no matter how inappropriate we may believe them to be. When you are dealing with difficult negotiations and ugly conflicts, it is not necessary to agree with the other side, but it is crucial to understand them.

As he reflected on what future generations might learn from this brush with disaster, Robert Kennedy described the crucial role of empathy, and the importance of taking the other side's concerns into consideration:

> The final lesson of the Cuban missile crisis is the importance of placing ourselves in the other country's shoes. During the crisis, President Kennedy spent more time trying to determine the effect of a particular course of action on Khrushchev or the Russians than on any other phase of what he was doing. What guided his deliberations was an effort not to disgrace Khrushchev, not to humiliate the Soviet Union.[6]

Empathy is needed most with people who seem to deserve it least. The more intolerable their behavior, the greater the potential benefit of understanding it.

CREATE SLACK

At the height of the crisis, soon after the quarantine was put in place, a Soviet ship came close to the line of interception. JFK decided against stopping the ship and having it boarded. Instead, he let it pass, taking the advice of an ExComm member who pointed out the possibility that the quarantine line had not yet been communicated to the ship's crew. The thinking was that perhaps it would be better to give the other side some time to think through and understand the consequences of their actions. Similarly, during the crisis, before an American U-2 spy plane was shot down over Cuba by a Soviet missile, the ExComm had decided that any such action would be cause for an immediate US military attack. According to Secretary of Defense McNamara, an action such as firing on Americans "would represent a decision by the Soviets to escalate the conflict. And therefore, before we sent the U-2, we agreed that if it was shot down we wouldn't meet—we'd simply attack."[7] However, when a spy plane *did* get shot down, the president ignored military leaders who advised immediate retaliation. It might have been an accident, JFK reasoned: Khrushchev was unlikely to have ordered such an attack when tensions were so high. *Perhaps it would be better not to assume the worst of intentions too quickly.* It turns out JFK's assessment was correct, and the order had not come from Khrushchev.

One way to reduce the risk of dangerous escalation is to create greater slack in the trigger for retaliation. Instead of punching someone the moment he pushes you, it may be useful to first figure out whether it was really a push, whether it was intentional, and what the reason was. If your antagonist keeps shoving you, or if you are sure it was deliberate and ill-intentioned, then a physical response might be appropriate (although there are, of course, other options). More generally, while it may be useful to have thought about the precise conditions under which you will retaliate, it is also important to leave some room for discretion. During the crisis, JFK reduced the likelihood that a mistake or misunderstanding would lead to escalation by giving some benefit of the doubt to the other side and by making sure they understood what lines were not to be crossed. If, instead, JFK had insisted on retaliating after even a single perceived transgression, the conflict would likely have escalated to dangerous levels.

Create slack. If your calculus for retaliation ignores the possibility of mistakes or misunderstanding, the risk of unhealthy and inappropriate escalation increases.

STRATEGIC FLEXIBILITY VS. CREDIBILITY

Slack does not come without cost. The greater the slack in the system, the more likely it is that you are seen as weak or irresolute if you choose not to retaliate. This could provoke even greater aggression if the other side is ill-intentioned or opportunistic. At a fundamental level, there is always a trade-off between *strategic flexibility* and *credibility*. In pursuit of flexibility, President Kennedy risked losing credibility each time he gave the Soviet Union the benefit of the doubt.

Credibility—the degree to which others believe that we will follow through on our commitments—helps us convince others to behave appropriately. *Strategic flexibility*—the option of changing our minds if sticking to a previous commitment seems unwise—allows us to make the best choice at the moment of decision. We typically want as much credibility *and* flexibility as possible. However, the more we invest in strategic flexibility, the less credibility we will typically have, and vice versa. For example, committing publicly to a strategy increases your credibility but reduces your flexibility because it is harder to back down. Private commitments provide greater flexibility, but signal less credibility and commitment.

There is almost always a trade-off between maintaining strategic flexibility and safeguarding credibility.

AVOID CORNERING YOURSELF

There will be times when you feel that losing some credibility is acceptable because following through on an earlier commitment (e.g., a deadline or ultimatum) would be disastrous. In other instances, you might decide that you must stick to your commitments, even if doing so is costly. In my experience, while it is impossible to completely eliminate the trade-off between strategic flexibility and credibility, it can be managed more or less wisely. You can avoid many such conflicts if you follow a simple rule: do not make ultimatums that you do not intend to follow through on, and absolutely avoid making ultimatums if you can achieve your objectives without them. In other words, to the extent possible, ultimatums should not be used unless they are both necessary and real.

Do not make ultimatums unless you plan to follow through on them—and even then, look for other means of influence that won't sacrifice strategic flexibility.

DON'T FORCE THE OTHER SIDE TO CHOOSE BETWEEN SMART DECISIONS AND SAVING FACE

The same problem exists on the other side of the table; they too must navigate the tension between maintaining their credibility and changing their minds when it is the smart thing to do. This is why, from JFK's perspective, the risk was not that Khrushchev was evil or irrational. The risk was that even smart, reasonably well-intentioned people can fall into the trap of having to fight when the only other option is to back down and look weak. As a result, much of what guided JFK's strategy was an effort not to put Khrushchev in a position where he had to choose between those two options. As Robert Kennedy wrote in his memoir of the crisis:

> Neither side wanted war over Cuba, we agreed, but it was possible that either side could take a step that—for reasons of "security" or "pride" or "face"—would require a response by the other side, which, in turn, for the same reasons of security, pride, or face, would bring about a counter-response and eventually an escalation into armed conflict. That was what [the President] wanted to avoid.... We were not going to misjudge, or miscalculate, or challenge the other side needlessly, or precipitously push our adversaries into a course of action that was not intended or anticipated.[8]

Do not force people to choose between doing what is smart and doing what helps them save face.

BEWARE THE CURSE OF KNOWLEDGE

A few days into the crisis, once the "gradual" strategy had been decided upon, President Kennedy had to address leaders of Congress to give an update on what had been discovered in Cuba and what the United States planned to do about it. The session did not go well, as members of Congress lambasted the president's strategy as insufficient, too weak, and likely to embolden further Soviet aggression. The president and his team were understandably upset about this reaction. Robert Kennedy was among those who felt strongly that the ideas emanating from Congress were naïve, terribly short-sighted, and a danger to humanity. It was at this point that JFK said something to his brother that I find to be especially telling about the character of the president. As Robert Kennedy recalled:

> He was upset by the time the meeting [with congressional leaders] ended. When we discussed it later he was more philosophical, pointing out that the Congressional leaders' reaction to what we should do, although more militant than his, was much the same as our first reaction when we first heard about the missiles the previous Tuesday.[9]

As JFK pointed out, members of the ExComm had been given many days—behind closed doors—to think about the problem, to debate it, to change their minds, to sleep on it, and to grapple with the complexities of seemingly straightforward choices. It was after all of this that they had come to the conclusion that the aggressive approach was unwise, and that the gradual approach, however imperfect, was a better idea. The question JFK was asking his brother to consider was this: *How can we expect Congress to be, on day one, where it took us so many days to get?* Despite his own misgivings about the congressional reaction, JFK reminded his brother that they ought not to hold Congress to a higher standard than they held themselves.

JFK was essentially pointing to what social scientists have referred to as the "curse of knowledge." The "curse" describes the following phenomenon: *Once we know something, it becomes very difficult for us to understand what it feels like not to know it.* That is, once we have learned something, or reached a conclusion, we seem to lose the ability to put ourselves in the mind-set of someone who has not yet had that realization—even though we *were* that person not so long ago. The curse can derail even the best efforts of those who are in the right and well-intentioned: parents who are trying to motivate, teachers who are trying to educate, leaders who are trying to inspire, and negotiators who are trying to persuade. In all of these domains, we do ourselves no favors when we forget that what is obvious to us will not be so obvious to the other side, and that it does *not* mean there is something wrong with them.

Beware the curse of knowledge. Once we know something, we lose the ability to understand what it feels like not to know it.

DON'T JUST PREPARE YOUR ARGUMENT, PREPARE YOUR AUDIENCE

The curse of knowledge reminds us that, as deal makers and diplomats, we ought not to simply walk into the negotiation with a set of prepared arguments that we hope will win the day. We also have to prepare our audience for our arguments. We need to think about what the other side needs to have seen, felt, experienced, or understood *before* they will even be receptive to the merits of our arguments and perspective. The greatest of arguments, the best of proposals, and the wisest of ideas will still fall short if we have not brought them to a point where they are capable of hearing, understanding, and evaluating what we say.

Don't just prepare your arguments, prepare your audience for your arguments.

Each year, the Program on Negotiation at Harvard University presents a Great Negotiator Award. The recipients have ranged from diplomats, to corporate deal makers, to artists. At some point during the Q&A that takes place on the day of the event, the recipient is inevitably asked to address the following question: *What are the characteristics of a great negotiator?* Having heard a dozen award recipients answer this question—people who have negotiated across many different cultures and in very different contexts—something stands out. There is one trait that everyone has mentioned in some form or another: *empathy.* Whether you are negotiating a business deal, an ethnic conflict, a job offer, a spousal dispute, or an international trade deal, it is *essential* that you try to understand how others see the situation.

By exploring the other side's perspective, we expand the set of options for de-escalating conflict and achieving mutually acceptable outcomes. It is not always easy. There will be times when the other party's actions leave little doubt that they are up to no good—meanwhile, your situation is precarious and getting worse by the day. How is empathy supposed to help you then? In the next chapter, we consider precisely such a situation, and take a look at how negotiating with empathy can work wonders.

14

LEVERAGING THE POWER OF EMPATHY

Deal Making with a Gun to Our Head

I WAS HELPING A CLIENT—a US-based technology venture—negotiate a commercial agreement (CA) with a company in China.[1] The two companies already had a different agreement in place; one year prior to my involvement, they had signed a "Joint Development Agreement" (JDA). According to the terms of the JDA, the Chinese company would provide cash for further development and testing of our technology, and would also start working towards the design of a manufacturing facility for the product. In return, our company would give them early access to our product and work with their engineers to help them prepare for an eventual commercial agreement with us. There was no obligation on either party to sign a commercial agreement, but both sides saw tremendous benefit in working together.

The JDA was a road map with many milestones, each delineating specific responsibilities for one or both parties (e.g., providing data, sharing projections, making payments, etc.). When a milestone was achieved, the two sides would "sign off" on its completion and then move on to the next milestone. All was going well—until suddenly, it was not. At issue was Milestone 2.8, on which the Chinese company was suddenly refusing to sign off. This milestone required our side to report to them the results of ten tests of our product (efficiency, durability, etc.) by the end of July. We had done so, on time, and the results had been excellent. On nine of the ten tests, the results were significantly "above the bar." On the tenth test, the results were ever so slightly below the level we had set, but not enough to make any practical difference in the product. Each side had previously accepted milestones that were much further off the mark, so this should have been an easy sign-off. Of course, if the other side really wanted to quibble about the tenth test result, they could—and that is exactly what they had decided to do.

Normally, a delay or disruption in the JDA would not be an issue. In this case, however, the Chinese company's unwillingness to sign off immediately became a matter of grave concern for my client. This is because a few months earlier, when the client was negotiating with venture capitalists (VCs) to raise additional funds for the company, the client had agreed to include a rather peculiar provision in the term sheet (contract). One of the VCs was concerned that the high (almost $200 million) valuation the client was asking for relied heavily on everything going well and on the product coming to market on schedule. How to give the VC confidence that everything would work out in the coming two years? For reasons that must have made sense to the parties at the time, the client and the VC had reached the following compromise: if the company appeared to be on track in the coming months—*as measured entirely by whether the Chinese company signed off on Milestone 2.8 by the end of September*—then it would be worth $200 million; otherwise it would be immediately devalued to $100 million! In other words, $100 million of valuation rested entirely on getting 2.8 accepted.

Now, here we were in the first week of August, and the Chinese company was refusing to sign off on 2.8. When we pushed them to move forward on signing off 2.8, they told us that we should stop obsessing over JDA milestones and instead move on to finalizing a commercial agreement, arguing that "after all, the CA is what really matters." When we persisted, they said something that made matters even worse: "Let's set aside Milestone 2.8 and the JDA for now. Let's start negotiating the CA. *When we sign the CA with you, on that same day we will also sign off on Milestone 2.8.*"

Allow me to clarify two things. First, there was no connection between any JDA milestone and the commercial agreement, nor was there any previous discussion of linking the two agreements. Why, suddenly, would they make such a demand on *this* of all milestones? Second, linking the 2.8 sign-off with the CA was giving the Chinese company *tremendous* leverage on us. If not for their threat to delay sign-off on 2.8, our side was in an extremely strong position to negotiate a lucrative CA: we had no binding commitment to them, we had other parties who would be interested in a deal with us, and the Chinese company had already invested quite heavily in the relationship. Certainly, we preferred a deal with them, but we would have had a lot of leverage to safeguard our financial and strategic interests in the CA negotiations if not for Milestone 2.8. The other side now had a powerful trump card: delaying 2.8 until we agreed to their commercial demands was tantamount to holding hostage a whopping $100 million of valuation.

They had leverage, and perhaps they knew it. They were certainly acting like it. From our perspective, there was no chance that they had seen the term sheet we had signed with our VC. Nor did anyone think he would have ever shared the information, which of course was *theoretically* possible. But could it be that during the discussions with the Chinese counterpart over the previous few weeks, people on our side had signaled some special importance of 2.8, or had seemed too desperate? Certainly, that was possible. And now we had a serious problem. What to do?

WITHOUT MONEY OR MUSCLE

The situation created tremendous anxiety—and some anger—on our side. After a year of working together in good faith, our partner was now going to hold our company's valuation hostage to extract concessions on a commercial agreement. We seemed to have few options, and none of them were great:

> **One: Agree to focus on the CA.** We could start negotiating the commercial agreement (as requested by the other side) and hope to reach a final agreement before the end of September. A deal was certainly possible in four to five weeks, but this was risky, because we might end up making desperate concessions in late September if we still hadn't reached a deal.

> **Two: Be fully transparent.** Perhaps we were falsely assuming that the other side knew about our valuation problem or that they were ill-intentioned. Maybe they

were just slow on 2.8 because it seemed unimportant to them. If so, we could tell them about our situation with the investor, and ask them to sign the milestone so as not to cause problems for us. This too would be risky: they might have no bad intentions yet, but revealing to them that we were desperate for sign-off might make it tempting to use this as leverage.

Three: Play hardball and demand sign-off on 2.8. We could be more aggressive and threaten to walk away from the CA if there were no sign-off on 2.8. This was also a risky tactic for obvious reasons, and costly to the relationship. Besides, actually walking away would not help us with the devaluation problem.

Four: Negotiate with the VC. We could instead negotiate with the VC and try to get the devaluation clause removed from the term sheet. We could legitimately argue that it was no longer a good measure of our progress and could cost the company money.

Options One, Two, and Three were risky. Option Four, which we tried to pursue, was not yielding the results we wanted. The VC understood our problem but would not yet commit to changing the valuation clause. We kept up pressure on the VC nonetheless, hoping that, if push came to shove at the end of September, he might show some flexibility. Most people in the team agreed that we ought to pursue Option One—try to get the CA done—and hope for the best. There was a lot of frustration with the behavior of our "partner," but a deal was still worth doing.

But *maybe* there was another way out.

The issue, from my perspective, was that we did not really know which problem we were supposed to be solving. Put another way, we still did not understand *precisely why* they were refusing to sign off on 2.8. Certainly, we had two reasonable theories: (a) they were ill-intentioned and using it as leverage, or (b) they were just not focused on the JDA and legitimately felt it was time to shift to the CA. Could it be something else? We had tried asking them why they wouldn't simply give us sign-off on multiple occasions, but the response had always been a somewhat vague and not very compelling reference to the tenth test result. So, we decided to look elsewhere for answers. We brought into the discussion additional people from our own company who had touchpoints with the Chinese company, and asked them to brainstorm with us. *What are all of the possible explanations for their unwillingness to sign off on Milestone 2.8?* This more exhaustive search for answers yielded two additional possible motivations that we had not yet considered:

1. The real issue might be the *next* milestone, 2.9. This milestone stated that as soon as 2.8 was completed, a "clock" would start on the Chinese side. According to this clock, they had exactly 12 months to get their manufacturing facility ready for our product. *Was it possible that they were running behind schedule and were delaying the sign-off on 2.8 simply to buy time on 2.9?* If they were behind schedule, this would put a lot of pressure on their chief engineer. Incidentally, sign-off on 2.8 required signatures from three people in their company: the CEO, a board member, and the chief engineer. And it had been the chief engineer, the person we had assumed would be our champion in selling the test results to the board, who had been most reluctant to give the go-ahead.

2. Another possible explanation could be Milestone 3.1, a payment milestone. Milestone 3.1 would be reached quickly after 2.8, given the automaticity of 2.9 and the ease of accomplishing 3.0. When that happened, they would owe us another $2 million payment. *Was it possible that they were dragging their feet on 2.8 in order to delay making another payment?* The other side had, previously, complained about how often they had to write checks to us, especially since we seemed well enough funded and they still had no guarantee there would be a commercial agreement.

Not knowing which of these problems to solve—and the other side would not have admitted to having either of these motivations—we decided to solve them both. But solving all of *their* problems would not be enough. We also had to ensure that they would reciprocate by signing off quickly on 2.8. We went to them with a three-pronged proposal: (a) we would work with them on revising payment terms and the 12-month timetable, which we framed as a concession in return for not quite passing the tenth test; (b) in exchange, they would agree to delay the CA negotiations until there was sign-off on 2.8; and finally, (c) if we did not receive sign-off by September 15, our company would stop working with their company until 2.8 was signed off. In other words, we offered as much flexibility as we could possibly muster to address their needs, in exchange for setting aside the CA until the milestone was signed. It was a risky move, but they agreed. In the ensuing weeks, we reached agreement on an installment plan for payments, a revised timetable with their chief engineer, and offered some engineering expertise from our side to help keep them on track for the 12-month delivery date. The concessions were trivial compared to what was at stake with the valuation and the CA.

Within a matter of weeks, the parties seemed to be on the same page; relations were much improved, all sides felt that their concerns were being heard, and there was no more discussion of the tenth test. But one final crisis did appear. Progress on all of these fronts had taken us until September 27, and we still did not have final sign-off on 2.8. The delay now seemed to be merely bureaucratic: they did not have the people and paperwork in place for the appropriate sign-off. They promised to send the documents over within two weeks. What now?

That night we decided to use the last arrow in our quiver: *tell them everything.* We told their CEO about the devaluation trigger and that unless he gave us sign-off immediately, we would be in a lot of trouble. Why would we do that? Isn't this exactly what we did not want to risk telling him? I will return to our reasons for doing so shortly—it was not desperation. We told the CEO that although we could wait for formal documentation to come later, the very next day we needed to show to our VCs an email from him that unequivocally stated we had met the requirements of 2.8.

We even offered to write the text of the email for him; all he had to do was copy and paste it if he agreed. He sent the email the following day. The valuation was saved.

EXPLORE *ALL* POTENTIAL EXPLANATIONS FOR THE OTHER SIDE'S BEHAVIOR

When the other side has a lot of power and seems willing to engage in unscrupulous behavior, your options seem limited. That is the world we thought we were in. But we were wrong. There were a number of options that were not immediately apparent to us because we were making inaccurate assumptions about the underlying problem. The turning point for us came when we decided to shed the assumption that the other side was ill-intentioned and taking unfair advantage of us. Instead, we wiped the board clean (literally—we erased one of the whiteboards to make room for brainstorming) and asked the question: *What are all of the potential explanations for their behavior?*

It is crucial for deal makers to investigate what factors other than sheer incompetence or evil intentions might motivate the other party to behave in a manner that seems aggressive, unfair, unethical, or irrational. Of course, you might conclude after an exhaustive examination that they really *are* out to get you, but it is best not to start with that assumption. In many cases, there are other factors in play. In this case, although there was nothing honorable about holding up 2.8 to get better payment terms or an easier timetable, even members of our own team acknowledged that the other side might understandably feel justified in delaying another $2 million payment, given the sizable investments they had already made in return for so little from us. Similarly, as some folks on our side suggested, the engineer might understandably be concerned that the timetable for him was unrealistic from the start, and maybe he had little faith that we would give him a break later in the year if he was running behind schedule. He could be using the technicality of our tenth test as a way to buy time that he thought was legitimately owed to him. What mattered was not so much how legitimate these concerns might seem to us, but how they seemed to them. Once we could wrap our arms around the possibility that they had motivations other than pure greed, we had more options for potentially resolving the conflict.

Consider all potential explanations for the other side's behavior. Do not start by assuming incompetence or ill intent.

IDENTIFY THE BARRIERS: PSYCHOLOGICAL, STRUCTURAL, AND TACTICAL

Not every negotiation should end with a deal. If the best you have to offer the other side is worse than their alternatives, not reaching a deal is the right outcome. Not reaching a deal is tragic only when you are the right partners for each other and value could be created for everyone, but something is standing in the way of getting it done. Just as it is important to consider all of the factors that might motivate the other side, before entering any important negotiation, it is important to anticipate as well as possible all of the factors that might derail the deal. *What are the barriers to reaching agreement?*

Broadly speaking, there are three classes of barriers that negotiators ought to consider:

> ***Psychological Barriers:*** These are barriers that exist in the minds of people, such as mistrust, ego, disliking the other party, emotions, biased perceptions of fairness, and overconfidence.
>
> ***Structural Barriers:*** These are barriers that are associated with the "rules of the game" as currently established—e.g., time pressure, having the wrong parties at the table, the use of agents whose incentives are misaligned with yours, too much media attention, insufficient availability of information, other deals or agreements that are constraining your options, etc.

> ***Tactical Barriers:*** These barriers arise from behaviors and choices on either side, such as publicly committing to a position that is untenable, aggressive tactics that provoke retaliation, focusing too narrowly on one issue and failing to consider all of the interests of each party, choosing not to exchange information, and so on.

In complex negotiations and difficult disputes, you will never anticipate all of the barriers, nor are you likely to eliminate all that you see, but putting forth this effort may substantially increase your chances of success. Better to know, as soon as possible, whether you need to find ways to overcome mistrust, gather more information, bring other parties to the table, negotiate behind closed doors, or preempt the use of aggressive tactics, than to go in with the blind faith that deals that are good for all parties will always get done. The more carefully you evaluate all the challenges that you may face, and the more comprehensively you consider the various tools and tactics at your disposal for addressing them, the more likely that your deal-making efforts will succeed.

Early, and throughout the negotiation, audit the psychological, structural, and tactical barriers that may obstruct deal making.

WORK THE WHOLE BODY

Imagine that you are on the street and someone attacks you. If you feel that you must fight back to defend yourself, you might instinctively make a fist and punch at the attacker's head. In the heat of the moment, you might try to do this over and over again, using one instrument against one target. While natural, this may not be the most effective approach, especially against a competent attacker. Rather, you want to "work the whole body." Instead of focusing narrowly on one target, or using only one method of attack, more experienced fighters will consider all of their instruments (two hands, two feet, knees, elbows, nearby items that can be used for defense, and so on) and evaluate all potential areas that could be targeted.

The same is true in deal making and diplomacy. Effective negotiators *work the whole body* by considering all of the barriers they need to target and all of the instruments at their disposal for doing so. In our negotiations, we had to think through all of the potential *barriers* to getting sign-off, for example: their engineer's deadline, their CEO's perception that we did not deserve more money without a signed CA, and the devaluation provision in our term sheet. We also had to think carefully about all of the *levers* available to us for targeting these barriers, for example: renegotiating with our investor, bringing in others from our company to help evaluate the other side's motivations, changing their payment terms, using our technical resources to solve their engineering concerns, and our ability to threaten disengagement if they did not sign off soon enough. I do not think we would have succeeded if we had used only "hard" tactics (threatening to walk away) or if we had only tried "soft" tactics (offering to meet their needs on payment and timetable). We needed a strategy that effectively combined various tactics.

Work the whole body. Consider all the barriers, approach the problem from all directions, and use all the levers at your disposal.

IGNORE ULTIMATUMS

Dispassionately evaluating all possible explanations for the other side's hostile behavior and having the patience to work the whole body is not easy. It is especially difficult when the other side is lobbing threats and ultimatums along with their aggressive actions and demands.

Every so often, in big negotiations and small, we encounter ultimatums: statements such as "We will never . . . ," "Under no conditions can we . . . ," "You must . . . ," or "That's impossible." My own rule for dealing with ultimatums, in the vast majority of situations, is actually quite simple. Regardless of the type of negotiation or who made the ultimatum, I am most likely to respond *by simply ignoring it.* I will not ask the other side to clarify what they meant. I will not ask them to repeat what they said. Nor am I likely to respond or react to the ultimatum itself. Instead, I behave as if it were never said. The reason is this: a day later, a week later, or perhaps even months or years later, the other side may come to the realization that what they once said they could never do is something they *must* do, or that the thing they said they would never do is actually in their best interest *to* do. When that day comes, the last thing I want is for them to remember having said they would not do it—or for them to worry that I will remember them having said it! It will be much easier for them to change course and avoid sticking to their earlier ultimatum if it was never afforded any importance or attention by me. I do not want to be in a position where I am forcing the other side to choose between sticking to their ultimatum and doing what is best for them (and for me).

Of course, there is always a chance that their ultimatum is real. Is it dangerous to have ignored it? Not really. The fact is, if it is a real ultimatum, they will repeat it over and over again, in all kinds of contexts and in all sorts of ways. At some point, depending on my assessment of the person and the situation, I can decide to take it seriously and accept that this is a real constraint for the other side. But it is also the case that many of the ultimatums that get thrown about in negotiations do not reflect absolute "red lines" or deal breakers. Sometimes people are just angry or upset, and the words come out more aggressively than necessary. Sometimes the other side feels that they have been pushed around for too long and are now simply trying to assert some control. Sometimes, in cross-cultural negotiations especially, it is merely an error in how emphasis was translated, or there may be differences in how assertively people tend to communicate. Sometimes they are just trying to underscore that this is an important issue for them, or are trying to extract greater concessions from you. In all such cases, ignoring the ultimatum helps avoid a situation where both sides end up constrained by the words of the other party.

Ignore ultimatums. The more attention you give to them, the harder it will be for the other side to back down if the situation changes.

REPHRASE ULTIMATUMS

There is also a variation on the "ignore ultimatums" strategy that is quite useful. Sometimes, before I ignore the ultimatum, I take just a moment to *rephrase the ultimatum as a non-ultimatum.* For example, if someone says "We can't possibly do X," I might respond with the following: "I can understand how, given where things stand *today,* this would be *difficult* for you to do . . ." By doing that, I've turned their completely rigid statement into something that is slightly more flexible. It now gives them at least two ways out if they eventually decide that doing X would be wise. By acknowledging that they are constrained "given where things stand today" (not forever) and that it would be "difficult" (not impossible) for them to move, we have left open the option of doing X at a later date, or under slightly different deal conditions.

Reframe ultimatums. By rephrasing ultimatums using less rigid language, you make it easier for the other side to back down later.

WHAT IS NOT NEGOTIABLE TODAY MAY BE NEGOTIABLE TOMORROW

Situations change and new opportunities sometimes emerge. What is not possible to achieve today may be possible to achieve in the future—but you have to be prepared to take advantage of the opening. Recall that even our best efforts at addressing the other party's concerns did not completely solve our problem; with only a few days left before the deadline, we had to tell their CEO exactly why we needed sign-off on 2.8. Why did we do that? Was it because we were now desperate and had no other choices? No. In fact, even with only three days left, we were not *that* desperate because we had already taken the steps necessary to ensure that he would not be able to use our need for 2.8 against us in the CA negotiations. This was part of our strategy from the start: because we had anticipated the *possibility* of one day needing to reveal our predicament to the CEO, we had demanded that CA negotiations be delayed until *after* 2.8 was signed off. As a result, there had been no progress on the CA for over a month and the parties were many weeks away from being able to conclude a CA. Now, with only three days left before our deadline, there was no way for the CEO to use our weakness to extract value in the commercial agreement. The only reason for him to delay signing off on 2.8 at this point would be if he just wanted to hurt us for no material benefit to himself, hardly something he would want to do with his future partner.

We were able to safely use our one remaining option—full transparency—only because we had carefully navigated our way to this potential endgame. From the first strategy session in early August, and throughout the negotiations, we never lost sight of the fact that the reason they had leverage on us was *not* that we needed them to sign off on 2.8. They had leverage on us because we needed sign-off *and* they had the ability to use this information to squeeze us in the CA negotiations. If we could take away that ability, which we did by delaying the CA negotiations, there was no way for them to use 2.8 as leverage against us once the deadline was near.

In negotiations of all kinds, it is crucial to keep an eye on how the strategic environment will develop over time—and how you can shape its development. Remember: *What is not negotiable today may be negotiable tomorrow.* A tactic that makes no sense to use early in the negotiation may be safe or profitable in the future. Your strategy or analysis from day one may be irrelevant by day two. What the other side could not agree to a week ago may now be acceptable. How they see the world tomorrow may be different from how they see the world today.

How the other side approaches a negotiation is not only *likely* to change over the weeks, months, and years ahead; it can also *be shaped* by the actions you take. We encountered a similar idea earlier, in the case of the Cuban Missile Crisis. As JFK reminded Robert Kennedy, it may not be possible to get Congress to agree with our course of action today, but that does not mean their perspective cannot be changed in the days or weeks ahead. Similarly, in our deal with the Chinese company, although we felt it was too risky to be transparent on day one, we could afford to do so a month later because we had changed the other side's ability to extract concessions from us. We see the same insight in the National Hockey League CBA negotiations of 1992. Although the players' success that year came at the cost of future relations, it does highlight the importance of timing in negotiations. The players understood that *when you negotiate can be as important as how you negotiate:* instead of issuing a strike at the start of the season, they waited to use the tactic until the alternatives of the other party were relatively weaker.

It is not enough that we start out with an understanding of all the parties and their perspectives; we also need to keep track of whether and how these might change or be influenced over time.

What is not negotiable today may be negotiable tomorrow. Think about how to shape incentives and options for all sides to make future attempts at negotiation more successful.

Of course, it is possible that your attempts at understanding the other side's perspective merely confirm that the other side is hell-bent on its point of view. There are times when the other side's perspective is so deeply entrenched that it is unlikely to change and is not amenable to influence. In the next chapter, let's consider such a situation and see some of the ways deadlock might still be overcome.

15

YIELDING

Selling Modernity in Saudi Arabia

THE YEAR WAS 1965, and King Faisal of Saudi Arabia had a problem. Still new to the throne, he was already waist-deep in his efforts to institute much-needed financial and social reforms for the country. One element of these reforms involved making available "innocent means of recreation for all citizens." As part of this agenda, King Faisal wanted to introduce television to Saudi Arabia. The only problem was that not everyone in the kingdom believed that the television was as innocent a technology as it pretended to be. Many religious conservatives considered the TV to be the work of the devil, which, depending on the kind of zealot with whom one was discussing the issue, could refer to either pitchforks and horns or stars and stripes. In any case, significant religious opposition to the technology was expected. How do you convince people that television is not an instrument of the devil's campaign? Luckily for Faisal, he was not the first king of Saudi Arabia to run into this problem—his father had seen similar troubles.

The year was 1925 and Ibn Saud was king. He was a powerful ruler who had, in fact, been the one to consolidate the kingdom of Saudi Arabia. He also had the support of the clergy. Yet, Ibn Saud had a problem. He wanted to introduce the country to modern technology—in this case, telegraph and telephony. The difficulty, as you might have guessed, was that in the eyes of some influential and religiously minded individuals, the only rational explanation for electromagnetic communication was Satan. How much of this was a real fear and not simply a means to obstruct modernization is difficult to assess. In either case, the king realized it would be difficult to make any technological progress without overcoming the clergy's concerns, regardless of whether these were deeply held or merely for public consumption. What now?

WITHOUT MONEY OR MUSCLE

Ibn Saud decided that the only way to tackle religiously expressed objections would be *through* religion itself, not by going around it. So, he invited a group of religious leaders to the palace and asked one to hold a microphone while another was asked to stand at the receiving end of the technology. He then asked the first to read a passage from the Quran, the Muslim holy book. As the voice was carried over to the speaker on the other end, Ibn Saud made the argument that would win the debate: if this machine were the work of the devil, how could it possibly carry the words of the Quran?[1]

Ibn Saud must have been pleased with how things worked out, because a quarter-century later, in 1949, he used the same argument when introducing radio stations in Saudi Arabia. To quell concerns that the devil's hand was on the radio dial, a recitation of the Quran was the first broadcast to be aired. Perhaps coincidentally—or maybe as a tactic to further co-opt the religious angle—the inauguration was scheduled for the Haj (Muslim holy pilgrimage) season.

Faisal could have done a lot worse than to take a page out of his father's playbook. In 1965, amidst concerns and protestations, the first television broadcast in Saudi Arabia included the recitation of the Quran,[2] thereby setting the world record for the number of times a member of the same family had been called upon to beat the devil out of high tech.[3]

YIELDING

I am a big advocate of seeking to control the frame early in the negotiation. When that is not an option, I advise reframing the negotiation as soon as possible. But sometimes neither is an option. Sometimes there is already a dominant frame, a well-established lens through which one or more of the parties are viewing the situation. You may be walking into a protracted negotiation or conflict where the parties have a deeply rooted perspective on the issues and their options. This could be the case in a family-business negotiation, in ethnic conflicts, or even in environments as benign as those that might exist in healthy, long-running business relationships with vendors, customers, or partners. Sometimes, the dominant frame is not based on a specific history of interactions between the parties, but rather reflects the influence of culture or other contextual factors.

In such situations, it may be too difficult or time-consuming to get people to abandon or change their perspective. Reframing may not be an option. As the TV/radio/telegraph examples demonstrate, when all else fails, you can sometimes overcome resistance to your ideas and proposals by *yielding*—that is, understanding and co-opting the other side's frame or perspective to make it work for you. In this case, when it became clear that technology would not be judged as effective or ineffective, but rather as good or evil, the king decided to stop resisting the frame and, instead, adopted it and reengineered it for his own use. That meant ensuring that his preferred outcome was packaged in such a way that it aligned with prevailing views on how "goodness" ought to be measured. Yielding is a principle that is often discussed in the martial arts: the idea is that there can be tremendous power in *going with*—and perhaps redirecting—rather than resisting the energy or attack that is coming your way. Likewise, in negotiations, yielding means "going with," and not "giving in." Doing so effectively requires a clear and unbiased understanding of how the other side views the situation, and of the metrics they will use to evaluate ideas and options.

Sometimes the best response to a deep-rooted perspective is to yield to it: understand it, adopt it, and repurpose it to advance your position.

BRIDGING TO ACCOMMODATE COMPETING PERSPECTIVES

Sometimes there is not one dominant perspective but two equally strong philosophies competing for dominance. This can be the case when each side has strong views on the correct way to discuss or evaluate issues, and they have seemingly incompatible ways of looking at the problem. In such a case, one potential solution is *bridging:* finding a way for one side to adopt the other's frame without losing leverage, or proposing a new frame that they can both safely adopt.

Not so long ago, I was speaking to the principal of a private school who was dealing with a conflict regarding teacher pay. Teacher salaries had always been set primarily on the basis of tenure—the more years you had worked, the more you were paid. Now, a group of wealthy donors to the school were demanding a change. The donors wanted performance-based pay rather than tenure-based pay, and they put forth proposals that would tie some amount of teacher pay to things such as student test results and teacher evaluations based on class visits by the principal. The teachers were unwilling to move in this direction, arguing that tenure was the right thing to reward because those with more years of experience were better teachers. The donors, meanwhile, were stuck on the idea of "performance-based" pay. The principal could understand each side's point of view, but they were talking past each other, unable to move beyond the idea of "performance-based" versus "tenure-based" pay. No one was ready to discuss the actual details of any proposal. What to do?

My suggestion was to put forth the idea that, actually, there is *no disagreement* between the two sides on the appropriate basis of pay. When examined closely, it is obvious that teachers *agree* that "performance-based" pay is the correct approach. The only difference between the two sides is how best to *measure* performance. Indeed, the teachers had constantly stated that those who bring more value to students should be paid more—this sounds like a performance-based argument—but they just happened to believe that "number of years" is the best measure because it is unbiased, unlike a principal's subjective evaluation. Donors would agree that tenure is the easiest to measure, and also that experience usually makes teachers better, but they would disagree about the extent to which tenure and effectiveness were correlated. If the principal could get the two sides to acknowledge that "performance-based" is not only an acceptable logic, but in fact the *only* logic either side has ever articulated (without necessarily having used those words), both sides might be able to overcome deadlock on the *logic* of teacher pay, and start discussing the *substance*. For example, what are the trade-offs when choosing between different measures of performance—and are these acceptable?[4] Is there a combination of measures that all sides could live with? Undoubtedly, the parties would still need to grapple with how much weight to put on different measures, but acknowledging that there is already consensus on the lens with which to view the problem might help the parties get past their current, somewhat ideologically driven, intransigence on starting principles.

Competing perspectives can be bridged if (a) one side can adopt the other's frame without sacrificing their ability to articulate key demands, or (b) both sides can agree to a new frame that gives neither an advantage.

YIELDING TO THE OTHER SIDE'S PERSPECTIVE CAN ENHANCE YOUR LEVERAGE

Sometimes the best way to convince someone of your point of view is to talk to them in their own language. Not only is this more efficient, but it can make your arguments even more powerful. There is something quite compelling about being able to demonstrate to someone that your demands remain legitimate "even if we accept your preferred logic for how to approach the problem." Indeed, King Faisal was likely on stronger ground than even he would have initially sought when he shifted from a "technology" frame to a "religion" frame. Likewise, teachers might have a greater impact on donors and other stakeholders if they can articulate their position in terms of the *need to identify appropriate bases of measuring performance* as opposed to the *legitimacy of tenure,* because the latter can be perceived as a merely self-serving or ideological stance.

Yielding to the other party's frame or perspective might enhance your leverage.

GIVE THE OTHER SIDE CONTROL—WITH CONDITIONS

Yielding to the other side, as risky as it is for the reasons we considered when discussing the importance of controlling the frame, can sometimes be the right strategy. A few years ago, we were negotiating a complex deal with a multibillion-dollar corporation that is a household name around the world. The company I was advising had been founded only a few years earlier but was growing quickly. The other side made clear that one of their key demands was a notification clause: we would have to inform them of all acquisition offers that we received in the coming few years and would have to give them time to make a counteroffer. Their concern was understandable: they did not want to wake up one day and discover we had been bought out by someone who might not want to continue the important relationship we were structuring.

Yet, this condition would impose potentially costly constraints on our future ability to sell the company at the best possible price. For example, if this partner wanted to buy us—a likely possibility—they would know whether we had other suitors and when other bidders increased their bids. Depending on the way the provision was written, it might also deter other potential acquirers from making offers in the first place. After a number of our revisions to their proposal were turned down for various, and sometimes vague, reasons, we decided to take a different approach. Instead of making any further proposals, we told the other side that we would allow them to craft absolutely *any* notification provision they wanted in order to protect their investment *provided that* it conformed to two principles: it would have to preserve both our ability to *find the highest potential bidder* and our ability to *extract the highest possible price* in a future acquisition scenario. If those conditions, which were hardly unreasonable, were met, we would accept whatever provision they crafted. If they could not meet these conditions, we would have to reject their proposal.

With the ball in their court now, and with our requirements made clear, the other side both softened their language and proposed new variants. With the proposal not coming from us, they were no longer in a defensive posture. What they finally came up with was acceptable to both sides and the deal moved ahead. The basic principle we were following was one that I sometimes advocate when there are legitimate concerns on both sides of the table and progress has been slow: *Give the other side control, but clarify your conditions.* This simple strategy:

- shows empathy for their concerns, allowing them to focus on finding solutions rather than continued advocacy;
- clarifies for the other side what is and isn't important to you, making their life easier;
- keeps either side from "owning" and clinging to its preferred idea or approach;
- helps find a solution by encouraging multiple, and often creative, proposals.

If your proposals are being rejected but their concerns seem legitimate, try giving the other side the task of structuring the deal—but clarify the conditions they must meet.

In most of the negotiations we have considered so far, we have focused on the importance of understanding the party on the other side of the table. But there may be *many* parties and *many* tables that are relevant to achieving your objectives. For example, in our negotiations with the Chinese company, we also had to consider the perspective of the VC; in the Cuban Missile Crisis, the ExComm had to understand the perspective of the Soviet Union but also consider Cuba; James Madison had to structure a process that would yield better outcomes not only in Philadelphia but also in the many debates to follow in the various states. In the next chapter, we look at the importance of understanding the points of view of *all* the parties that are relevant to the negotiation. Effective negotiators take all players into account.

16

MAP OUT THE NEGOTIATION SPACE

Negotiating the Louisiana Purchase

FEW WILL CLAIM TO have ever heard of the *Preliminary and Secret Treaty between the French Republic and His Catholic Majesty the King of Spain, Concerning the Aggrandizement of His Royal Highness the Infant Duke of Parma in Italy and the Retrocession of Louisiana.*[1] And yet, this treaty, signed between France and Spain in 1800, would soon play a very important role in history. On the basis of this agreement, Spain returned to France the vast Louisiana Territory in North America that France had ceded to Spain in 1763 after France was defeated in the French and Indian War.

During the negotiations between Spain and France, Napoleon's ambassador allegedly gave "the most solemn assurances" that France would not sell or cede the Louisiana Territory to any other country, but rather would return it to Spain if France wanted to dispossess it. When Napoleon decided to turn around and sell the land to the United States, it came as a surprise to the Spanish, the Americans, and even many in France. In 1803, the United States bought the Louisiana Territory from France for approximately four cents an acre. With the Louisiana Purchase, the United States doubled in size, acquiring land that would make up all or some of 15 future states.

The Spanish were furious, claiming that "the sale of this Province to the United States is founded in the violation of a promise so absolute as that it ought to be respected," and asked the United States to "suspend the ratification and effect of a treaty which rests on such a basis."[2] The Americans interpreted this as little more than a reason to speed up ratification and get the deal done before things unraveled. The United States Minister to France, Robert Livingston, reported to Secretary of State

James Madison: "I should have mentioned to you that I have strong reasons to believe that the Spanish cession contained an agreement not to part with Louisiana to any other power, this I have thro' a channel that I think I can rely upon, and tho' it will not affect our right it should hasten your measures in availing yourselves of the Treaty."[3]

While the question of whether France had the right to sell has been debated by historians for a number of reasons, Madison found the Spanish argument weak: "The promise made by the French ambassador, that no alienation should be made, formed no part of the Treaty of retrocession to France and if it had, could have no effect on the purchase by the United States, which was made in good faith without notice from Spain of any such condition."[4] More importantly, the Americans were convinced that the Spanish would not attempt to stop the sale by force. A bigger problem for the United States was the potential for seller's remorse on the part of France, as evidenced by French efforts to seemingly add last-minute conditions and to complicate and delay closure.[5] Indeed, Napoleon had long wanted to keep the territory for France. As he explained: "I have proved the importance I attach to this province, since my first diplomatic act with Spain had the object of recovering it. I renounce it with the greatest regret: to attempt obstinately to retain it would be folly."[6] Why then did Napoleon part with the Louisiana Territory?

WITHOUT MONEY OR MUSCLE

Why would the *French* sell land claimed by the *Spanish* to the *Americans*? Simply put, because of the *British*. France was at war with England. If all went exactly as planned, France could deal with the British as well as take possession of Louisiana. This was not looking likely. A slave revolt against the French in what is now the island of Haiti and Dominican Republic—along with bad weather that kept French ships stuck in the icy waters of Europe—depleted resources necessary to stave off the growing threat from England. To make matters still worse for the French, there was a risk that if they tried to hold on to Louisiana, the United States would decide to ally with England against France. This is because the Louisiana Territory included New Orleans, which was of great strategic importance to the United States. Having it in the hands of Napoleon caused tremendous anxiety for the Americans. In a letter to Robert Livingston, President Thomas Jefferson wrote:

> The cession of Louisiana and the Floridas by Spain to France works most sorely on the U.S.... Of all nations of any consideration France is the one which hitherto has offered the fewest points on which we could have any conflict of right, and the most points of a communion of interests. From these causes we have ever looked to her as our natural friend, as one with which we never could have an occasion of difference. Her growth therefore we viewed as our own, her misfortunes ours. There is on the globe one single spot, the possessor of which is our natural and habitual enemy. It is New Orleans, through which the produce of three-eighths of our territory must pass to market, and from its fertility it will ere long yield more than half of our whole produce and contain more than half our inhabitants. France placing herself in that door assumes to us the attitude of defiance. Spain might have retained it quietly for years.... Not so can it ever be in the hands of France ... these circumstances render it impossible that France and the U.S. can continue long friends when they meet in so irritable a position. They as well as we must be blind if they do not see this; and we must be very improvident if we do not begin to make arrangements on that hypothesis. The day that France takes possession of N. Orleans.... From that moment we must marry ourselves to the British fleet and nation.... This is not a state of things we seek or desire. It is one which this measure, if adopted by France, forces on us, as necessarily as any other cause, by the laws of nature, brings on its necessary effect ... [France] does not need [Louisiana] in time of peace. And in war she could not depend on them because they would be so easily intercepted. I should suppose that all these considerations might in some proper form be brought into view of the government of France.... If France considers Louisiana however as indispensable for her views she might perhaps be willing to look about for arrangements which might reconcile it to our interests. If anything could do this it would be the ceding to us the island of New Orleans and the Floridas. This would

> certainly in a great degree remove the causes of jarring and irritation between us. . . . It would at any rate relieve us from the necessity of taking immediate measures for countervailing such an operation by arrangements in another quarter. . . . Every eye in the U.S. is now fixed on this affair of Louisiana. Perhaps nothing since the revolutionary war has produced more uneasy sensations through the body of the nation.[7]

The American delegation went to negotiate with the French. To their surprise, they were received by a delegation from Napoleon that wanted to sell the *entire* territory. There was clearly more behind this offer than a need to keep the United States from siding with England, which could have been accomplished simply by giving up New Orleans. The single biggest factor in Napoleon's decision may have been his fear that the entire Louisiana Territory could be taken by the British if France was defeated in war. Better to give it to the Americans than to the British, reasoned Napoleon—and if doing so empowered the United States and gave the British more to contend with in the future, all the better. As Napoleon explained to one of his ministers: "I shall not keep a possession which will not be safe in our hands, which will perhaps be the cause of a clash with the Americans or perhaps make them cold towards me. On the contrary, I shall use it to bind them to me, to cause them to break with the British, and I shall create enemies against the latter who shall one day avenge us. My mind is made up. I shall give Louisiana to the United States."[8]

The Americans were suddenly being offered more than they had expected, or had even prepared to negotiate. After finalizing the deal in an improvised process with dubious constitutional authority, James Monroe wrote to James Madison:

> Could we have procur'd a part of the territory we shod. never have thot. of getting the whole; but the decision of the consul was to sell the whole, and we cod. not obtain any change in his mind on the subject. So peculiarly critical too was the moment, owing to the pressure of Engld. . . . that it seemed indispensable, to turn these several circumstances to our account, to meet this govt. on the scale it proposed & conclude a treaty with it on the terms we have without delay. I have no question or rather doubt of the advantage of the bargain to the

> UStates.... I shall not be surprised to hear that many of those who were ready to plunge into a war for a light portion of what is obtained, shod. now take another course and declaim agnst the govt. & its agents for getting too much. But the clamour will not avail them. It will disgrace them. We have obtaind more of what they professed to wish, than they had an idea of, and at a much less price, than they were willing to give for the little portion they expected to get.[9]

And so it was that the greatest land deal in history took place between a country that had questionable legal authority to sell and another that had questionable legal authority to buy.

THINK TRILATERALLY

The outcome you achieve will be a function of how carefully you consider the roles of *all* parties that are affecting a negotiation. A common mistake in negotiation is to think about relationships *bilaterally*—that is, to focus only on your relationship with the party across the table from you. For example, during the negotiations, the Americans could have evaluated only the dynamics of the US–France relationship. In this way of thinking, the United States might have imagined that the French would offer nothing, or at best, be willing to cede only New Orleans. They might also have assumed that if acquiring New Orleans were possible, it would be costly because Napoleon valued that possession highly.

As we have seen, the negotiation analysis changes when parties think *trilaterally:* evaluating not only the relationship that the parties have with each other, but the relationships each has with other parties. Once we consider the relationship between England and France, the behavior of the French becomes less surprising. It is even more understandable when we further consider the relationship between the United States and England vis-à-vis the French.

Of course, we can go further and discuss the value of "quadrilateral" or "pentagonal" analysis, but the basic point remains the same: the folly is to consider only the relationship—and to imagine only the possibilities—that exist in the direct relationship between the parties at the table. Negotiators who consider the role of third parties and assess their impact on those who are at the table are better equipped to anticipate the behavior of the other side and to strategize optimally.

Think trilaterally: evaluate how third parties influence or alter the interests, constraints, and alternatives of those at the table.

MAP OUT THE NEGOTIATION SPACE

When I advise on deals or conflicts, one of the first things I do in our strategy meeting is ask my client to map out the *negotiation space.* The negotiation space consists of *all parties that are relevant* to the negotiation. By "relevant" I mean one of two things: (a) any party that can influence this deal, and (b) any party that is influenced by the deal. If there are parties that can influence the deal, I will want to consider whether, when, and in what capacity we or others might benefit from bringing them in to the process (or from keeping them out). If there are parties that are influenced by the deal we are negotiating, I also want to keep an eye on them, because they are likely to have an incentive to make moves that could impact our strategy and outcomes.

In the case of the Louisiana Purchase, the negotiation space consisted not only of the United States, England, France, and Spain, but also the people who were actually making the decisions. Companies and countries don't make decisions, people do. Napoleon is not the same as "France." The negotiation space also consisted of lawmakers in the United States who might facilitate or obstruct the deal, and the slaves in Haiti and their oppressors, because any change in the outcome of that revolt could influence whether France still feared losing the war to England. The more you "zoom out" to see the negotiation in the broader context, the more accurate will be your understanding of the other side's likely behavior, and the more likely you are to wisely revise your strategy when relevant events take place elsewhere in the negotiation space. Meanwhile, a failure to map out and analyze the negotiation space leaves you vulnerable, because you miss opportunities when they arise, and you are unable to see all of the barriers you face or all of the levers available to you.

Map out the negotiation space. Your strategy should take into account all parties who can influence the deal or who are influenced by the deal.

ICAP ANALYSIS: INTERESTS, CONSTRAINTS, ALTERNATIVES, AND PERSPECTIVE

When it comes to understanding the other parties in the deal, what precisely are we to understand about them? I have developed a framework (ICAP) to help organize your thinking around four critical factors: each party's interests, constraints, alternatives, and perspective. Here are the kinds of questions that each of these raises:

- **Interests:** What do the other parties value? What do they want and why? What are their relative priorities? Why are they doing this deal? Why now rather than last month or next year? What do they worry about? What objectives are they trying to achieve with this negotiation? Are their interests likely to change over time? If so, how?
- **Constraints:** What are the things they can and cannot do? On which issues do they have more or less flexibility? On which issues are their hands completely tied? What is causing them to be constrained? How might their constraints change over time? Are there other parties with whom we might negotiate on their side who would be less constrained?
- **Alternatives:** What happens to them if there is no deal? Are their outside options strong or weak? Are their alternatives likely to improve or deteriorate over time? How might their alternatives be shaped?
- **Perspective:** How are they seeing this deal? What is their mind-set? Where does this negotiation fit into the portfolio of deals they are doing? Is this a high or low priority for them? Are they thinking strategically or tactically? Long-term or short-term? Is this negotiation occupying a large or small portion of their organization's attention?

An ICAP analysis at the outset of negotiations—and updating the analysis as the deal progresses—can be crucial. The better you understand their *interests,* the more likely you will be able to structure deals that create value for all parties, and to overcome deadlock. Understanding *constraints* is important because there will be times when even the concessions you deserve will not be possible to obtain because the other side's hands are truly tied in those areas. In such cases, you will be more likely to achieve your objectives if you know what is and is not achievable, and which type of deal structure is actually viable. The more carefully you have assessed their *alternatives,* the better you understand the value you are bringing to the table, and the leverage that you have. Finally, when you understand the *perspective*—psychological, cultural, or organizational—with which they are approaching this deal, you are better positioned to anticipate the types of barriers that might emerge. You are also more likely to take the steps that can help reshape their perspective to one that may be more amenable to effective and productive deal making.

ICAP Analysis: Assess the interests, constraints, alternatives, and perspective of all parties in the negotiation space.

THE ACTION AWAY FROM THE TABLE

James Sebenius and David Lax, authors of *3D Negotiation,* highlight the importance of tactics that take place "away from the table." As they correctly and comprehensively illustrate, there are often times when your ability to influence the deal through direct engagement with the other side is limited. In such cases especially, it becomes crucial to consider the role that others in the negotiation space might play in your strategy. As in the case with US interests in the Louisiana Territory, one's greatest source of leverage may have nothing to do with traditional measures of power (US willingness to go to war with France), and everything to do with the dynamics elsewhere in the negotiation space (heightened French fears caused by a slave revolt in Haiti and bad weather in Europe).

The lesson of the Louisiana Purchase may have been even simpler for 19th-century Americans: just wait for the British to scare the wits out of your enemies and be there to gather the spoils. The French were not the only ones to fall victim to this dynamic. In the aftermath of the Crimean War (1853–56), in which Russia had been defeated by an alliance that included England, France, and the Ottoman Empire, Tsar Alexander II began to fear that he might lose control of Russia's Alaskan territory in a future war with England. Like Napoleon a half century earlier, the tsar reasoned that it was far better for the land to go to the Americans in exchange for some cash than to the British in exchange for nothing. When substantive negotiations were finally conducted in 1867, the Americans agreed to purchase the land. Not to be outdone by his predecessor, Secretary of State William Seward made the purchase of the vast region for a price of two cents per acre.[10]

When it comes to evaluating the action away from the table and how it can influence the negotiation, there are three assessments worth making:

> ***Static Assessment:*** How does the *existence* of third parties influence the interests, constraints, alternatives, and perspectives of all parties in the negotiation?
>
> ***Dynamic Assessment:*** How is third-party influence *changing* over time? That is, are the other side's alternatives improving or worsening? Are constraints tightening or loosening? Are interests evolving?
>
> ***Strategic Assessment:*** How might we engage with third parties to *influence* the negotiation? Might they be willing to put pressure on the other side? Might they agree to subsidize the deal? Would doing a deal with a third party change the power dynamics in our favor?

Sometimes, we can leverage the existence of third parties to achieve our objectives (static). Other times, our success hinges on anticipating a changing landscape (dynamic). And then there are situations where we must actively engage with third parties to create the conditions for success (strategic).

Your analysis and approach should take into account the static, dynamic, and strategic possibilities of leveraging third parties.

BE PREPARED FOR GOOD FORTUNE

It is not entirely obvious whether the US negotiators were thinking trilaterally and had a great strategy, or whether they simply got lucky. While some have lauded this deal as President Jefferson's greatest contribution to the United States, and others have fawned over the remarkably low price negotiated by the Americans, there are less adulatory interpretations of the event as well. President Jefferson's political nemesis, Alexander Hamilton, saw the outcome as having more to do with good fortune and opportune timing than with astute bargaining:

> This purchase has been made during the period of Mr. Jefferson's presidency, and, will, doubtless, give eclat to his administration. Every man, however, possessed of the least candour and reflection will readily acknowledge that the acquisition has been solely owing to a fortuitous concurrence of unforseen and unexpected circumstances, and not to any wise or vigorous measures on the part of the American government.... To the deadly climate of St. Domingo, and to the courage and obstinate resistance made by its black inhabitants are we indebted for the obstacles which delayed the colonization of Louisiana, till the auspicious moment, when a rupture between England and France gave a new turn to the projects of the latter, and destroyed at once all her schemes as to this favourite object of her ambition.[11]

Hamilton may have had a point. But that does not mean the opportunity, when it arose, could not have been bungled. Sometimes, you deserve credit for having updated your strategy effectively in real time as the impact of distal elements in the negotiation space came into focus. Sometimes, the most important thing a negotiator can do is to be logistically prepared, politically organized, and psychologically ready to seal the deal if and when the stars align and the timing is right. If the groundwork for a deal has not been laid in anticipation of a window of opportunity that might eventually open, that opportunity could be lost. The earlier one conducts a comprehensive analysis of the negotiation space and the sooner one assesses all of the levers that can be pushed and pulled to shape the deal, the more likely is success, even when the endgame is not visible at the outset.

Prepare for good fortune. Be psychologically, organizationally, and politically prepared in case a window of opportunity opens for deal making or diplomacy.

IMPROVE POSITIONING AND CREATE OPTION VALUE

When the negotiation space is large, the road ahead is long, and a path to agreement is difficult to envision, negotiators often feel that "prepare for good fortune" is just a nice way of saying "wait until you get lucky." As a result, they adopt a short-term, tactical approach to deal making and fail to create the conditions necessary for achieving long-term objectives. The underlying assumption is that it is useless to strategize when the future is uncertain and too many factors are out of your control. This is a mistake. When reaching agreement seems a distant hope and nothing you can do today will guarantee success, it is useful to instead think about how you can *improve positioning and create option value.*

To *improve positioning,* we audit the weaknesses in our current negotiation capability and take actions to chip away at those problems. This way, we are better positioned for deal making should an opportunity arise. For example, we might need to bolster our outside options, build coalitions, strengthen the value of our offering, build trust, and so on.

If the problem is that we have limited strategic options (e.g., too few paths that can lead to success), we might invest in *creating option value:* taking costly actions today that will generate additional degrees of freedom in the future. For example, you might create back channels with a terrorist organization even when there is no appetite for negotiation and you are waging an aggressive military campaign; this is costly and risky, but it creates the option of negotiating in the future if your calculus changes.

To appreciate the value of improving position and creating option value even when there is no agreement in sight, consider the deal-making process that resulted in the acquisition of basketball star James Harden by the Houston Rockets. In a simple trade, you would make one move: for example, give the other team some of your players in exchange for receiving your preferred player.[12] But if you don't have what the other team wants, you might need to make a few moves to first improve your position. In the case of the Houston Rockets, in a strategy that unfolded over *five years* and involved *14 separate moves,* General Manager Daryl Morey built up the necessary assets—the right mix of players and draft picks—to acquire James Harden from the Oklahoma City Thunder. When it came time to make the deal in 2012, Houston was able to offer Oklahoma City two players (one acquired via trade, and the other by a draft pick that was itself acquired via trade), a first-round draft pick belonging to Dallas, a first-round draft pick belonging to Toronto, and a second-round draft pick belonging to Charlotte. When it was over, Houston had acquired one of the best young talents in the league.

Not even Daryl Morey, who negotiated the deal, knew exactly where all of the moves would eventually end. Signing Harden was *one* possible endpoint, but there were other potential plays and opportunities that could have arisen on the basis of the preparatory maneuvers. So was it just luck? Or was it a perfectly crafted strategy? Neither. Thinking back to his role, Morey reflected on how he improved his positioning and created option value to increase the likelihood of a successful outcome:

> With each transaction, I look to put the odds in our favor as much as possible both on the move made at the time but also for the myriad of possible outcomes in the future. Each move in the Harden trade was made with the end in mind of trading for a superstar of Harden's caliber. Each move worked together to increase not only the value of what we could trade but also the mix of what we could trade. By the end, we had players that could help a team win now or in the future. We had draft picks

> in different range of risk/reward. We could save a team significant room on the salary cap. Salary cap savings ended up not being part of the trade but we were ready if it was.... Once you accept that you don't have all the answers and the job is just to shift the odds in your favor, it really opens up great things such as this trade.[13]

Just because the future is uncertain and there is much you cannot control does not mean you cannot adopt a strategic, long-term perspective. In especially difficult and protracted negotiations, you have to be willing to make wise sacrifices in the short run, and even to take steps that seem counterproductive except for the fact that you are keeping an eye on how today's gambits will help you create and exploit future opportunities.

When there is no possibility of reaching a deal today, prepare for future opportunities with moves that improve positioning and create option value.

DON'T RUSH TO EMBRACE A WINNING STRATEGY

As we have discussed, some people respond to complexity and uncertainty by assuming that having a strategy is useless. Others make a different mistake: they rush to embrace a strategy *earlier than is necessary or wise.* This happens even when there is no objective reason to sacrifice strategic flexibility, and when it makes sense to keep multiple options open. In my experience, when multiple options are on the table (e.g., different strategies, or a choice among doing different deals), and continued discussion has failed to identify a clear winner, there comes a time when people are tired of deliberating and there is a psychological need for closure. As a result, an interesting and potentially dangerous shift takes place in the room: as soon as there is some degree of momentum behind one of the options, people stop discussing the pros and cons of each option rationally. Instead, they begin to overweight factors that favor the currently preferred option and to selectively seek out "cons" for the option that has less support. This reflects what psychologists have called the *confirmation bias.* Because people want to be able to devote their enthusiasm and entire attention to one approach, and to start implementing it, they no longer evaluate all options as fairly or comprehensively as they should.

There is an added organizational factor that compounds the psychological bias. Different strategies, or different types of deals, often require you to employ different resources, bring different people on board, and expend different kinds of social and political capital. As a result, once you go too far down one path, it becomes difficult to switch. There comes a point when there is simply too much organizational momentum and too much strategy-specific investment towards one course of action; a change is psychologically, organizationally, and politically difficult.

During the Cuban Missile Crisis, President Kennedy was adamant that no options be discarded a moment sooner than necessary. Even after it was clear that the gradual strategy (quarantine, coalition-building, and negotiation) was wiser than the aggressive option (military strikes), the president asked that each option continue to be refined *as if* it were to be the chosen strategy. In fact, until the very last moment that JFK went on national television to announce the course of action he planned to pursue, he had two speeches fully prepared for him in case any last-minute information or analysis suggested they were pursuing the wrong strategy. Based on documents that were made available to the public only a few years ago, had a change in strategy been necessary, the following would have been the opening lines of his address:

> My fellow Americans, with a heavy heart, and in necessary fulfillment of my oath of office, I have ordered—and the United States Air Force has now carried out—military operations with conventional weapons only, to remove a major nuclear weapons build-up from the soil of Cuba.[14]

Until the absolute last moment, the president was prepared psychologically, organizationally, and politically to change course if a wiser approach could be identified.

Avoid picking a winning strategy earlier than is necessary. Keep options open and be prepared—psychologically, organizationally, and politically—to change course.

In this chapter, we looked at complex environments where there is much that you cannot control. As we have seen, even in the face of uncertainty, it is possible to strategize effectively; you can improve your position, create option value, and keep all options on the table until you have greater clarity or are forced to choose. We have also seen that you are more likely to overcome deadlock and resolve conflicts if you map out the negotiation space, think trilaterally, and consider how to leverage the action that takes place away from the bargaining table.

Even so, sometimes the hardest situations are not the most complex. Sometimes a situation is difficult *because* it is so simple: the negotiation space is already well understood, and no one else is going to swoop in to save the day or provide you the leverage you need; there is no option of preparing for good fortune because time is up and, to make matters worse, the other side holds all the cards and they are not in the mood to treat you nicely. Your options are few, none of them are good, and they are getting worse. What levers do you have then? How does empathy help you here? Let's find out.

17

PARTNERS, NOT OPPONENTS

Caught in the Crossfire

NOT SO LONG AGO, a successful entrepreneur who was a student of mine ("Sam") found himself at the tragic end of a true reversal of fortune.[1] It had all started out so well. A year earlier he had received a call from one of the largest retailers in the United States, asking whether he would be interested in earning some extra revenue. There was no catch. The retailer had decided to switch suppliers for one unique type of apparel, and the new supplier was an overseas Asian company. The retailer had never worked with this Asian company before and reached out to my student for help. Sam already had a good business relationship with the retailer, and although he did not know the Asian company either, he was very familiar with the manufacturing landscape where the company was located. The retailer wanted Sam's company to act as an intermediary between them and this Asian company. For almost no work at all other than coordinating the purchase and sale of product, he would get a percentage of each transaction that took place. If all went well, Sam's company stood to make over a million dollars each year—a sizable amount of money for him.

The celebrations did not last long. Just a few months into the relationship, Sam received a letter from a US manufacturer. The letter claimed that in making this apparel, the Asian company had violated the US manufacturer's patent. Given the nature of the relationship between the parties, the US manufacturer was suing the retailer, the Asian company, and Sam. The US manufacturer was open to settling out of court, but was demanding a huge settlement. Legally, the retailer was in a very safe position and had no incentive to negotiate. For practical reasons, the Asian company could not easily be made to pay through litigation. This left only my student squarely in the crosshairs. And the US manufacturer was going to come at Sam with everything they had—because this wasn't just about patent infringement. The US manufacturer had been the original supplier of this apparel to the retailer until the Asian company had come into the picture and undercut them on price. They were not happy.

Sam did not want to pay millions in a settlement, but he also did not want to go through a legal battle. He decided to reach out to his allies in this mess, in the hope that one or both of them would be willing to chip in money to help settle the matter. The retailer was very sympathetic and felt bad that Sam had been dragged into this, but while they offered to vouch for him in legal proceedings, they were unwilling to offer any money. The Asian company argued that there was no patent infringement so there was no reason for them to offer money, an easy thing for them to say given they were outside the reach of the law. He was on his own. He asked his lawyers to reach out to the US manufacturer and explain that although he was clearly innocent in this matter, he was willing to settle for a few hundred thousand dollars, a goodwill gesture aimed at helping everyone avoid court. It did not work. They went to court.

After seven months and $400,000 in legal fees, the court ruled in favor of the US manufacturer. Sam was asked to pay almost $2 million, which was more than four times as much as he'd made in the deal before it had come to a halt due to the lawsuit. His only options now were to pay the money, to appeal the decision, or to try again to settle out of court. Paying up would be extremely costly. An out-of-court settlement would be even harder now than it had been last time, given the US manufacturer's legal victory. The lawyers believed an appeal made the most sense, but they did not pretend his chances were good. Which route to take? You've already lost once in court, the other side has the leverage, you are facing a multimillion-dollar loss, none of your allies are coming to your aid, and the party on the other side of the dispute seems out for blood. What now?

WITHOUT MONEY OR MUSCLE

As Sam tells the story, he was sitting around one day when the thought came to him: *What would my negotiations professor advise?* It did not take long to come up with an answer. *Look for the value-maximizing outcome.* In other words, given the interests, constraints, and alternatives of all the parties, what approach or outcome would create the most amount of total value in this situation? *Before worrying too much about how you will get there, first figure out what the optimal deal would be.* So he started to map out the negotiation space and think this through.

In the very beginning, the **retailer's** relationship with each of the three parties had been as follows:

	Relationship with Retailer	Product to Sell	Best Partner for Retailer
US Manufacturer	Good	Expensive	YES
Asian Company	None	Cheap	No
Student	Good	None	No

After the Asian company undercut the US manufacturer with the help of my student, the situation changed:

	Relationship with Retailer	Product to Sell	Best Partner for Retailer
US Manufacturer	Good	Expensive	No
Asian Company	None	Cheap	No
Student	Good	None	No
Asian Company + Student	Good	Cheap	YES

Once the Asian company's patent infringement was revealed, and after the US manufacturer sued the other three parties, things changed again. The US manufacturer's relationship with the retailer was now bad, and the Asian company's product was no longer viable for sale in the United States.

	Relationship with Retailer	Product to Sell	Best Partner for Retailer
US Manufacturer	Bad	Expensive	No
Asian Company	Bad	None	No
Student	Great	None	No
Asian Company + Student	Unclear	None	No

The value maximizing outcome was starting to come into focus. The US manufacturer had the power to squeeze money out of Sam, but there was an even bigger pot of money that was now missing from the entire equation: no one was capable of selling any product to the retailer. The lawsuit could yield a few million dollars for the US manufacturer, but many more millions in value were being destroyed because no one had the necessary combination of assets: a good relationship with the retailer *plus* a product to sell. But there was one possible entity that could bring both assets to the table: it would be a *partnership between the US manufacturer and Sam.* Might this work?

Sam called up the CEO of the US manufacturing firm and told him that he was getting on a plane to come and see him. "I have an idea I'd like to share with you. If I can't convince you in 20 minutes, I will fly right back." The CEO agreed to meet. On the way to the meeting, my student also called up his contacts at the retailer to share the broad outlines of what he planned to propose. They gave him the go-ahead to try to structure such an arrangement.

In the CEO's office, Sam explained his analysis and the idea. The retailer would never buy directly from a company that had sued it, but the manufacturer's patented product was a good one and there was no substitute supplier. Sam had a good relationship with the retailer, not to mention the retailer felt they owed him for putting him through the terrible ordeal. Sam could be the intermediary between the manufacturer and the retailer. The manufacturer would have to make a few concessions to the retailer to smooth things over, but a deal was possible. The two sides crunched some numbers, haggled a bit, and then came to the following agreement: (a) Sam would pay the manufacturer a few hundred thousand dollars upfront, partly to reimburse the manufacturer's legal costs; (b) Sam would become the exclusive intermediary between the manufacturer and the retailer—this would be worth a couple million dollars to his company in the coming years; (c) Sam would become the exclusive distributor for the US manufacturer for overseas sales—another valuable win for him.

All three parties signed off, and the reversal of fortune had been reversed once more.

PARTNERS, NOT OPPONENTS

When someone sues you, how are you likely to view them? Most people would see that person as an enemy, or at least as an adversary. This is understandable, but potentially dangerous, because we tend to think and act differently based on how we view the person on the other side of the table. We typically have lower tolerance, less hope, and a reduced willingness to engage constructively with our enemies. And this tendency can be costly—to us and to them.

In the martial arts dojo where I practiced, it was not uncommon during class to hear students ask questions such as: What if your opponent is bigger? What if your opponent grabs you like this? What if your opponent…?

Such statements always invited a caveat by our instructor. "They are partners, not opponents," he would correct his students any time they used the word "opponent" to describe the person they were practicing with in class. "Remember that the people you are sparring with are there to help you learn. How will you learn from them if you think of them as opponents?" Often, he would take it a step further: "Even the person who attacks you on the street is your partner. How will you remember to stay calm, or attempt to resolve the situation without fighting, if you think of him as an opponent?"

The same is true in deadlocks and in ugly conflicts. As my student's experience illustrates, it can be dangerous to see others one-dimensionally, and especially to label them as an opponent or enemy. If you pigeon-hole someone based on their prior behavior, you may miss opportunities that emerge when the game changes. In this case, the US manufacturer started out a stranger, turned into an adversary, and ended up an ally. The Asian company went from being a strategic asset to a legal liability in a matter of months. The biggest obstacle to solving Sam's problem may have been the inability—at first—to see that situations change and that people can outgrow their labels.

Labels might provide an efficient means of describing someone ("she's my competitor"), but they are necessarily incomplete and limiting. It is always best to remember that the people you are dealing with are not competitors, allies, enemies, or friends—they are just *people* who, like you, have interests, constraints, alternatives, and perspectives (ICAP). As a negotiator, your job is to understand these factors and to address the situation accordingly. In my negotiating, I still find it useful to retain the label *partner* for everyone (whether they are acting like a "friend" or "foe"), because it reminds me to have empathy, to be open to the possibility of collaboration in even the most difficult relationships, and to shed assumptions about what is or is not possible.

See the other side as your partner, not your opponent, regardless of the type or degree of conflict. It is hard to empathize or collaborate with "opponents."

LOOK FOR WAYS TO CREATE VALUE

In the world of business, negotiators often talk about "creating value." It is a reminder that there may be ways to improve the deal for everyone, or at least to improve it for some people without hurting others. Deal makers should obviously try to improve agreements and create more value. After all, would you rather be arguing over how to share $100 or $200? It is easier to find a solution, not to mention more profitable, when there is more to gain from reaching a deal, or more to lose from no deal.

The same principle holds in all negotiations—that is to say, in all areas of human interaction. Negotiators should be in the business of creating value whether they are bargaining over deal terms, facing deadlock, or addressing an ugly conflict. In relatively simple situations it is easy to see what is necessary to create value. For example, in the NFL or NHL, you create value when you end a strike or lockout because only by playing games can you bring money into the system (from viewers, advertisers, etc.) that you can share. To achieve this, you need to solve some difficult problems, such as agreeing on revenue split, but now you have clarity on the direction in which you should move.

It's not so easy when the situation is complex: when there are many parties, many divergent interests, competing intuitions about the right strategy, or a lack of clarity or consensus on what the goal should even be. For example, it was not obvious what Sam should have been even trying to accomplish. Minimize the cost of settlement? Find a way to win in court? Appeal to the manufacturer's goodwill? Leave it to the lawyers? Find a way to pressure the Asian company?

In such situations, an effective way to clarify objectives and choose between options is to ask: *What would be the value-maximizing solution?* Focusing on this principle immediately helped shift the student's attention to the idea that it might be possible to make everyone better off, and that it was unwise to start off assuming the conflict was a zero-sum situation. Thinking in terms of value creation also helped to increase the set of visible options. For example, creating a business relationship with the person who is suing you is not intuitive, unless you are dispassionately looking to create value in every situation. Here again, we see the value of regarding all other parties as *partners, not opponents,* in the process. When you see them as your partner, you are more likely to identify and implement value-creating solutions to the problem.

Start by asking: What would be the value-maximizing outcome? Are there ways to create value?

FIRST, IMAGINE THE IMPOSSIBLE

One of the reasons people fail to focus on unlocking value is because the situation seems impossible. They are already so sure there is no *good* solution that they fail to consider the possibility of a *great* one. This type of thinking can sometimes be changed. One of my executive students was the president of his family business. His father, who owned 90% of the business, was still heavily involved, although he had officially retired. After years of conflict over matters big and small, the son had decided to talk with his father about how to move forward given the bad and worsening situation. The father was constantly overriding the son's decisions and getting involved in matters where he did not have enough information. He was also making it difficult for the son to get out of his shadow and be seen as a legitimate president in the eyes of employees and customers. The conversation was likely to be ugly. It had come to the point where the son felt he would have to leave the business or ask his father to step away, and no matter what, he expected there to be anger, resentment, and potentially, a worsening of the conflict. He was dreading it. He was unsure how to start the conversation, which issues to bring up, or what outcome he even preferred.

When I heard his story and his prediction of disaster, my first question was this: Is there any possibility that both of you will walk away from the conversation *happier* than you had been before talking? He was quiet. He then told me he had never even considered the possibility. I said to him, "Imagine a world in which both of you are glad that the conversation happened. And now paint me a picture. What would that world look like?" And then the conversation changed. He started talking about how his father might be feeling as he thought about his retirement after decades of building a business. He spoke with regret about how little time they spent together outside of work because neither of them wanted another fight. He wondered whether his father was also longing to have this conversation. He was still not sure what the right solution would be, but he was much more confident that he would be able to go in with an open mind and have a potentially value-creating conversation. I do not know how this particular story ended, but before he left the executive program to go back to his business, the student told me that he was looking forward to seeing and talking with his father.

The same approach can also help when you are facing intransigence. In business deals, for example, when the other side says something cannot be done, or that they are unable to accept our request, I might say to them as I did to my student, "Imagine a world in which you were able to say 'yes.' And paint me a picture. What would that world look like?" This helps shift the conversation from what cannot be done to why it cannot be done. There are times, especially when an agreement seems unlikely, when even the people saying no have not carefully thought through exactly what would allow them to accept what is currently unacceptable. Of course, sometimes this conversation still leads to a dead end. But other times, they bring up concerns or obstacles that we are actually able to address in ways they would not have anticipated. At the very least, we get clarity on what needs to change if we want to revisit the possibility of a deal in the future.

Ask people to imagine a world in which the seemingly impossible actually happens. Then ask them to paint you a picture of what that world looks like.

By seeing the other side as a partner rather than an opponent, by focusing on the principle of value creation, and by pushing others to challenge their own assumptions about what is possible, you increase the possibility of breaking deadlock and resolving ugly conflict. Of course, you might still need to knock down barriers, manage the process, help the other side sell the deal, and so on, but you will have a better understanding of where you are going and the steps you need to take.

I end this section with some thoughts on what many would consider to be the ugliest of situations—those that are rife with long-standing mistrust, deep hostility, and a protracted history of grievances. We will consider some of the reasons why extremely divergent perspectives can persist, sometimes for generations, and how we might change our approach and perspective when dealing with seemingly intractable conflicts.

18
COMPARE THE MAPS

Lessons in Cartography and Linguistics

IT HAS BEEN ARGUED that the oldest maps may have been those that humans used to chart out celestial bodies, rather than features of the earth, but maps of earthly terrain have been with us for thousands of years. Their benefits are many, but perhaps the most basic of these is that they help us navigate terrain with which we are not intimately familiar. As such, maps serve as conduits of knowledge, allowing those without expertise to benefit from the efforts of those who came before them. Today, these representations of reality are everywhere: in our cars, on our phones, and in our heads. And they can get us into trouble.

I was born in the United States, but when I was five, my family moved to India for a few years. As a result, I spent some of my early school years there, returning to the United States when I was nine. When I started school again in the United States, I confronted the range of issues anyone would be expected to encounter when entering or reentering a different country: social, academic, and cultural. But then there was the problem that seemed to defy categorization. For quite some time, I puzzled over something that made no sense to me. Simply put, why was it that no one in the United States knew what the map of India looked like? Hanging on the walls, published in textbooks, and printed on globes in the classroom, the world looked like I had always known it—except when it came to the country in which I'd just spent almost five years.

UNDERSTANDING THE IMPOSSIBLE

Imagine for a moment, if you're from the United States, that you traveled to Europe or Asia for the first time and discovered that every map of

America was missing Florida, or perhaps Texas, or Maine, and that no one else seemed to be confused or bothered by this. In my case, a significant portion of northern India had been seemingly chopped off the country. It looked—*weird.*

Eventually, the realization dawned. In almost every other country in the world, the state known to Indians as "Jammu & Kashmir" includes a vast region (Kashmir) that is considered disputed territory. And here lies the problem. Of course, every Indian knows that there is a dispute *in* Kashmir. It's just that the rest of the world believes the dispute *is* Kashmir. Then I realized that people in Pakistan, the other country with a heavy involvement in the Kashmir dispute, had probably spent their lives looking at a very different map than I had.[1]

The problem I encountered decades ago as a kid is far from unique—and the world getting flatter and more connected in recent years has so far done little to improve matters. In 2010, *Washington Monthly* published an article titled "The Agnostic Cartographer," which gave a peek into how one of the most popular of all mapmakers, Google Maps, decides what the world should look like. In researching a story about how a technical glitch caused Google Maps to inadvertently reassign disputed territory in India (Arunachal Pradesh) as belonging to China, the author unearthed some fascinating facts:

> Google runs an entirely separate maps site, ditu.google.cn, for Chinese users, which operates within the great Chinese firewall. This isn't just a one-off concession to the party leaders in Beijing: Google maintains thirty-two different region-specific versions of its Maps tool for different countries around the world that each abide by the respective local laws.[2]

When Google first launched its Maps initiative in 2005, it announced to the world that "we think maps can be useful and fun." Sometimes, it turns out, they are neither. Of course, the problem extends beyond maps. What is true of cartography is no less true of the "facts" one learns about history; each has been vetted, often without conscious or explicit intent, by the self-serving, identity-protecting, culture-replicating biases of otherwise well-intentioned people and institutions.

From their earliest memories, people on all sides of a conflict—anyone who has ever opened a book, turned on a TV, listened to a speech, or picked up a newspaper—have grown up with their own, entirely different, and incompatible, rendition of reality.

Consider the case of language. The Cuban Missile Crisis is remembered for the many lessons it teaches policy makers, leaders, and negotiators. But it is not just why we remember the crisis, but how we remember it that can be important. So it is worth asking: Why do we call it the "Cuban Missile Crisis"? Why not call it something else? How about the "Caribbean Crisis"? Or, let's say, the "October Crisis"?

One reason seems obvious: "Cuban Missile Crisis" is more descriptive than alternative labels—after all, the conflict had to do with *missiles* in *Cuba*. But is there perhaps more to the story? The other two names I have suggested above were not arbitrarily chosen as options. Nor were they created by me. Where do you suppose they come from?

A moment's reflection might reveal that, in fact, these are the names that other countries have used to describe the same conflict. In Russia, the event is remembered as the *Caribbean Crisis*. In Cuba, it is the *October Crisis*. These different names reflect the differing narratives that surround the conflict in these two countries. From the Soviet perspective, the real problem had little to do with missiles in Cuba per se. The missiles were just one element of the broader Cold War conflict, which included, from the Soviet perspective, other equally important factors, such as the US missiles in Turkey, the mounting conflict in Vietnam, and the tensions in Berlin. Indeed, at the time, the Soviet Union and the United States had multiple crises, in many parts of the world—this was merely the one in the *Caribbean*. Meanwhile, from the Cuban perspective, there probably appeared to be a crisis with the United States every month or so; this one was the *October Crisis*, not to be confused with the crisis in January or February or any other month of the year.

Negotiators cannot deal effectively with conflict without seeking to understand the narratives that exist on the other side(s) of the table. Indeed, even the agreement that President Kennedy ultimately reached with Premier Khrushchev required an appreciation for the Soviet position that the missiles in Cuba could not be considered in isolation from the threat posed by US missiles in Turkey. But it is not merely in the moment of conflict, and in the service of negotiation, that competing narratives need to be acknowledged. An appreciation for the different ways in which the past can be remembered, recorded, and taught on either side of a dispute can also help *preempt conflict.* When preemption is not possible, such an understanding can at least inject a measure of humility and respect into negotiations between parties who disagree on almost everything.

THE SOCIAL CONSTRUCTION OF CONFLICT

When people spend their entire lives *knowing* the truth, they come to believe that anyone who disagrees with them is incompetent, ignorant, or up to no good. There is an alternative possibility. Maybe the other side was simply brainwashed—and so were we. Identities and interests are *socially constructed.* This can help explain not only the depth of conflict that can exist between countries, but also the hostile divisions that can emerge between competing political parties, different religious ideologies, pro-life and pro-choice advocates, labor unions and management, and even rival corporate entities. In all such environments, each side can come to see its own perspective as moral while others are viewed with suspicion and derision. The discrepancy can persist and widen because all sides pass judgment on events using their own self-serving standards of legitimacy.

Conflict between *people* may be natural, but conflict between *peoples* always has a strong socially constructed basis that defines its parameters and sustains it over generations. It may not be possible for either side, at least in the short run, to overcome or set aside the potentially incendiary influences of upbringing. Nor is this something that we can unequivocally say would be desirable—it may be that some of the same forces that fuel fear and disparagement of others also motivate value-creating activities inspired by cultural pride or the comfort that comes from an expansive social identity. What is possible, and essential for resolving conflict, is an acknowledgment that the other side considers its perspective just as legitimate as we consider ours, and for much the same reasons. Acknowledging this is not always easy, but the failure to do so makes it hard to justify engagement and easy to justify escalation of hostilities.

Protracted conflicts cannot be resolved without genuine efforts to understand the deep-seated forces that legitimize each side's perspective and behavior.

ASKING FOR THE SACRED

Consider one of the barriers to negotiated agreement between Israelis and Palestinians. In addition to the creativity and courage that is needed if leaders on both sides are to work out a solution to the many issues they face, for any peace process to be effective there will need to be an accommodation for the differing narratives that each side holds dear to the heart. The date celebrated as Independence Day (Yom Ha'atzmaut) in Israel is remembered as the Day of Catastrophe (Naqba) by Palestinians. Each side's narrative is based on the selective weighting of historic events and incongruous beliefs about who has suffered more, to whom the land really belongs, which rights are God given, and which issues ought to be negotiable.

What happens when, in this context, the prime minister of Israel demands that Palestinian recognition of Israel "as a Jewish state" must be a *precondition* to peace negotiations?[3] It is difficult enough to expect someone to make a concession that compromises what they consider to be their sacred beliefs or rights; asking them to do so before negotiations can even begin is particularly unhelpful. Even in more mundane negotiations—for example, a business dispute or spousal conflict in which both sides feel that the other party has acted worse—it is typically ineffective to ask the other side to make a costly, irrevocable concession upfront (e.g., admit to wrongdoing) before there is any guarantee that you also plan to make some costly concessions, or that the dispute can be ultimately resolved if sufficient concessions are made.

It is always best if a conflict can be resolved without requiring either side to make very costly concessions, but this is not always possible. Even when necessary, the demand for such concessions ought not to be rushed. In armed conflicts, business disputes, and family skirmishes, there may come a time—perhaps when the prospect of a lasting settlement becomes credible, or because there has been a long-lasting and mutually hurting stalemate—when parties will agree to do what was previously considered "unthinkable," or to make concessions on issues that were once deemed nonnegotiable. But it is usually a bad idea, and likely to be a deal breaker, if you start off negotiations with a demand for such concessions.

Understand what is sacred to the other side and avoid asking for it as a precondition to engagement. They might agree to negotiate what was once nonnegotiable, but only if they see a credible path to resolving the conflict or achieving vital objectives.

HISTORY BEGINS WHEN WE WERE WRONGED

Across protracted conflicts around the globe, parties of every race and creed are making demands that they truly believe are legitimate and just—and they are concluding that the other side is uninterested in legitimacy or justice because these demands are being rejected. But a refusal by the other side to agree to our demands, especially when we have failed to mention how *their* core concerns will be met, should not put into question their character or motivation. The problem is that what we consider to be the greatest injustice, or the highest moral imperative, or the first problem that needs addressing, is largely dependent on which history books are sitting in our library.

In *Great Hatred, Little Room,* Jonathan Powell recounts an event in which the clash of narratives underlying the Northern Ireland conflict came to the surface in somewhat colorful fashion. It was December 1997, and Martin McGuinness of Sinn Fein (the political partner of the militant IRA) was visiting 10 Downing Street, the official office and residence of the British prime minister. Upon entering the Cabinet Room, McGuinness remarked to Prime Minister Tony Blair, "So this is where all the damage was done." Assuming this was a reference to an IRA attack on the residence in 1991, Powell, the PM's chief of staff, started to go into some detail about the damage that was done by the attack. No doubt bemused by Powell's response, McGuinness clarified that he had not been referring to the damage caused by the IRA bombing six years earlier. He was referring to the damage caused by the *negotiations* that had taken place, in that very same room, between Irish Republican leader Michael Collins and then-Prime Minister Lloyd George, which had led to the partitioning of Ireland—*back in 1921.*

Sinn Fein's perspective that day, and throughout the ensuing years, was firmly rooted in the events that had taken place three-quarters of a century earlier, the last time Sinn Fein had been invited to 10 Downing Street. From Powell's perspective, one of the elements most essential for holding together the tenuous, but ultimately successful, peace process was a deliberate and persistent effort to bridge the gap between "our shorter-term perspective" and the other side's "longer sense of historical grievance."

I have witnessed such discrepancies in negotiations of all kinds: labor leaders typically have longer memories than management; the party that got less value in the last round of negotiation perceives the current negotiation as an opportunity to settle scores, while the other side takes a "rational" forward-looking perspective; employees will remember how their boss treated them in every previous encounter, while the boss will have to be reminded about even having met with the employee a few days earlier. History *typically* begins the first time I did the right thing or you did the wrong thing—not the other way around.

History begins at different times for different people. The dates that register on our calendars are typically those that mark our victories and victimizations.

DON'T ASK PEOPLE TO FORGET THE PAST

Ignoring such differences in the hope that everyone will come to terms with "current reality" and will be forward-looking in their behavior fails to appreciate the long and powerful shadow that the past casts on how people see their sense of self and purpose. Asking people to forget the past is not a very effective strategy. One religious leader discovered this in 1973, when, calling for peace in Northern Ireland, he instead gave rise to one of the enduring slogans of the violent resistance. In response to his impassioned appeal to the crowd that it was time to set aside what had divided them in the past and to get on with the future, someone shouted back, "To hell with the future, let's get on with the past!"

A wiser strategy may be to help people build a bridge between the past and the future. I have found it much easier to negotiate with someone when, instead of fighting about the importance of historic rights and wrongs, I have encouraged the idea of applying the lessons of the past to help deal with the current situation. If someone feels they have been wronged, the "lesson" may be that they should mistrust and perhaps retaliate against the wrongdoer—and that does not leave much space for negotiation. But sometimes the other side can be encouraged to embrace a different lesson: to ask for reparations, to ask for an apology, to make amends, to simply forgive, or to work together with the objective of ensuring that no future wrongdoings can or will be perpetrated. Each of *these* paths requires negotiation. Each requires that history be confronted, not ignored. Even if it were possible, it is not obvious that we should wish for a world in which everyone could forget historic conflict and wrongdoings. There might be no vengeance in such a world, but there would also be little inspiration or capacity for preempting future conflicts or working towards a stable peace.

Asking people to forget the past is futile, but it is sometimes possible to help them find more value-creating ways to apply the lessons of the past.

BUT LET US BEGIN

Not long ago, on a flight to India, I was filling out a customs declaration form. It asked most of the questions one would anticipate, including "Are you bringing the following items . . . ?" One of the items on the list was Prohibited Articles. Turning the card over to find out what was prohibited, I found, along with the usual suspects (narcotic drugs, counterfeit currency, etc.), something I did not quite expect: "Maps and literature where Indian external boundaries have been shown incorrectly."

So there it was—just one more barrier erected to keep people from finding out how others might see the world differently. Just another obstacle to bridging divergent perspectives and reaching greater understanding. Such maneuvers are *by no means* unique to one country. And that is the point. Among the most natural reactions to conflict is fear: the fear of internal dissent or disunity; the fear of being perceived as weak; the fear of being the only one who will decide to act with civility or to take a softer stance; the fear of being exploited. Such fear is natural, and understandable. But fear alone should not dictate the parameters of whether and how we engage with our enemies or adversaries. It is not the way forward if conflict is to be mitigated or resolved.

President Kennedy, in his inaugural address to the nation on January 20, 1961, focused much of his attention on speaking to erstwhile adversaries of the United States and offered his own advice on how to handle seemingly impossible negotiations:

> So let us begin anew—remembering on both sides that civility is not a sign of weakness, and sincerity is always subject to proof. Let us never negotiate out of fear. But let us never fear to negotiate.

Time and again we have seen that neither caution nor courage alone provides sound basis for human interaction. Both are needed. Engagement does not guarantee success in the short run, but a failure to engage almost always prolongs and worsens conflict. President Kennedy understood this all too well:

> All this will not be finished in the first 100 days. Nor will it be finished in the first 1,000 days, nor in the life of this Administration, nor even perhaps in our lifetime on this planet. But let us begin.

Never let fear dictate your response to the problems of human interaction.

SUMMARY OF LESSONS FROM PART III: THE POWER OF EMPATHY

- Empathy expands the set of options—for you.
- Empathy is needed most when dealing with people who seem to deserve it least.
- Create slack. Your calculus for when to retaliate or escalate should accommodate mistakes and misunderstanding.
- There is a trade-off between maintaining strategic flexibility and safeguarding credibility.
- Don't corner yourself with unwise or unnecessary ultimatums and threats.
- Don't force the other side to choose between smart decisions and saving face.
- Beware the curse of knowledge.
- Don't just prepare your arguments, prepare your audience for your arguments.
- Consider all potential explanations for the other side's behavior; do not start by assuming incompetence or ill intent.
- Identify all the barriers: psychological, structural, and tactical.
- Work the whole body: target all barriers; use all levers.
- Ignore ultimatums.
- Rephrase ultimatums.
- What isn't negotiable today may be negotiable tomorrow—shape future incentives and options.
- Yielding means "going with," not "giving in." Understand, adopt, and leverage the other side's perspective.
- Bridge to accommodate competing perspectives.
- Yielding to the other side's frame might enhance your leverage.
- If necessary, give up control over proposing the solution—but clarify the conditions the other side must meet.
- Think trilaterally.
- Map out the negotiation space.
- ICAP analysis: what are the Interests, Constraints, Alternatives, and Perspectives of all parties?
- Your analysis should include the static, dynamic, and strategic possibilities of leveraging third parties.

- Be prepared—psychologically, organizationally, and politically—for good fortune.
- If reaching a deal today is impossible, improve positioning and create option value for the future.
- Don't pick a winning strategy too soon. Maintain options and strengthen your ability to change course.
- See the other side as partners, not opponents.
- Focus on creating value, no matter how ugly the conflict.
- "Imagine a world where this would be possible. Now paint me a picture."
- Understand the deep-seated forces that legitimize each side's perspective and behavior.
- Avoid asking for sacred concessions as a precondition to engagement.
- History begins when we were wronged.
- Don't ask people to forget the past—encourage them to find value-creating ways to apply its lessons.
- Never let fear dictate your response to problems of human interaction.

What we usually consider as impossible are simply engineering problems—there's no law of physics preventing them.

MICHIO KAKU

19

THE PATH FORWARD

I OFTEN REMIND MY STUDENTS that when they attend a course on negotiation, it does not make the world a better place. It does not make any of the people they will have to deal with in the future nicer, wiser, more sophisticated, or more ethical. *All we can try to do is equip you better for dealing with people who are no different than they were before you came to class.* This is why almost everything we teach is designed to be effective—to increase your likelihood of success—regardless of whether the other side has ever attended a course on negotiation.

The same is true of this book. Here, I have tried to assume the worst in the situations you will encounter: aggressive moves, deadlock, escalating conflict, lack of transparency, apparent ill intent, mistrust, and a lack of money or muscle to solve the problem. The hope is that as you navigate the seemingly impossible and the routine negotiations in your own life, the principles highlighted here will give you additional ideas and tools for resolving disputes, overcoming deadlock, and reaching better agreements and understandings.

Throughout the book I have highlighted the importance of being attentive to the nonsubstantive concerns that parties might have, of being mindful of process, and of deeply understanding the perspective of all the parties that are relevant to the negotiation. I conclude with one final story, which serves to remind us that effective negotiation requires sustained vigilance in all of these matters.

ANNOUNCING PEACE IN NORTHERN IRELAND

The ethno-political conflict in Northern Ireland dates back centuries, but its more recent manifestation took shape early in the 20th century. After Ireland won its independence from the United Kingdom, southern Ireland and northern Ireland were partitioned, with the north opting to remain separate from the Irish Free State, established in the south. The conflict was split along political and religious lines. Those who wanted freedom from the UK were known as Nationalists; they were primarily Catholic and in the majority, except in Northern Ireland. Those who wanted to remain a part of the UK were known as Unionists; they were primarily Protestant, and represented a majority in Northern Ireland. From the 1920s to the early 1960s, Northern Ireland continued its association with the UK, but with its own parliament—a situation that did not sit well with the Catholic Nationalists in the north, a minority that now faced systemic discrimination.

Conflict erupted in the mid-1960s, when a revived Irish Republican Army (IRA) began its armed campaign against the British state. Loyalist paramilitary groups formed to fight back against the Republican threat. Violence escalated, with almost 500 lives lost in 1972, the bloodiest year of the conflict. By the end of the century, close to 3,500 people had died, and over 100,000 had suffered physical injuries—in a country with a population under two million.

The peace process began with fits and starts in the mid-1990s. Over time, it became clear that while the IRA would not be given a seat at the table, a peace deal could not be reached without the involvement of Sinn Fein, a group considered by almost everyone to be the political arm of the IRA. In 1998, the UK, the Republic of Ireland, and eight political parties from Northern Ireland, including Sinn Fein, signed the historic Good Friday Agreement. The agreement created a devolved government in Northern Ireland with power sharing between the two sides to the conflict, and it established a number of overlapping institutions to bridge the interests of the Republic of Ireland, Northern Ireland, and the United Kingdom.

Problems remained, and the conflict would fester. In the years that followed, due in large part to the on-again, off-again progress on IRA disarmament, the parliament of Northern Ireland was repeatedly shut down, with Unionists withdrawing in protest over IRA intransigence. The British would rescind home rule in Northern Ireland, only to return it again when there was progress. Meanwhile, violence resumed between the two sides, albeit at levels significantly lower than those that had prevailed in previous years.

In November 2003, continued disaffection with the deadlock led to a defeat of political moderates in Northern Ireland. In came the more extreme Democratic Unionist Party (DUP, led by Ian Paisley) and Sinn Fein (led by Gerry Adams). If the moderates had failed to reach an agreement on disarmament and how to share power in practice, what hope was there with these two archrivals? When Ian Paisley was told by a reporter in 1997 that Gerry Adams was willing to sit down with him, he responded: "I will never sit down with Gerry Adams.... He'd sit with anyone. He'd sit down with the devil. In fact, Adams does sit down with the devil."[1]

Despite many setbacks, however, after parliamentary elections in Northern Ireland in March 2007, the two erstwhile enemies did meet face-to-face for the first time to conclude a power-sharing agreement. The *Guardian* described the event as follows: "The accord between the veteran unionist firebrand and the leader of a militant republican movement that once killed opponents was hailed in London and Dublin as the defining moment in 10 years of a protracted peace process."[2] In May 2007, direct rule of Northern Ireland by the British was ended when Ian Paisley (DUP) and Martin McGuinness (Sinn Fein) were sworn in as First Minister and Deputy First Minister, respectively.

While the meeting—and the peace it sought to herald—was centuries in the making, there is no reason for peacemakers to ever be assured that petty squabbling, one-upmanship, or last-minute demands will not derail the process. In the case of Paisley and Adams, thankfully, when that moment arose, some craftsmanship literally saved the day. Jonathan Powell describes what happened in his book, *Talking to Terrorists*: "When we reached the end of the Northern Ireland process and Ian Paisley had finally agreed to meet Gerry Adams, we remained blocked on one issue: where they would sit. Paisley wanted to sit opposite the Republicans so they looked like rivals rather than friends, but Adams insisted on sitting next to Paisley so they looked like equals and colleagues."[3]

Clearly, peace negotiators in Vietnam are not the only ones who get hung up on seating arrangements. How do you convince the parties to set aside this seemingly petty demand? How, with a deadline looming, do you persuade one of the parties to make the gracious concession? It turns out that you can't always do these things—some folks are a bit stubborn when they start seeing things as a matter of principle. So when all else fails, you have to get creative, and creativity is all about challenging your most basic assumptions. Powell explains how the deadlock was overcome: "We could not find a way through this blockage until a bright Northern Ireland Office official came up with the idea of building a new sort of table, diamond shaped, so they could sit at the apex, both next to each other and opposite each other at the same time."[4]

And that's how they solved it.

CREATIVITY AND VIGILANCE

I used to wonder why my children still have a mandatory woodworking class in their elementary school. I no longer do. When you enter the topsy-turvy world of ugly conflict, you come to appreciate every skill you have ever honed, every tool you have ever picked up, and every lesson you have ever learned. Preparedness, as we have seen, is indispensable, but no amount of preparation will obviate the need for creativity when the unexpected emerges. This should not be surprising; if there were off-the-shelf solutions to all problems, no problems would ever persist. Our ability to find unique solutions to our problems is greatly enhanced when we are skilled in using *all* of our sources of leverage—not just money and muscle, but also the powers of framing, process, and empathy.

Experience also builds an appreciation for the importance of constant vigilance; when you are in the domain of complex deals or protracted conflict, sometimes the most dangerous problems come disguised as issues of trivial importance. You never know when a seemingly simple matter will threaten to derail a deal that has been months or years in the making. Such problems—the kind you never saw coming—will stretch your capacity for problem solving and creativity. You will have to be prepared to think fast and flexibly, and to apply the principles discussed throughout this book as events are unfolding in real time. This does not mean that every problem should be treated as if it were a colossal impediment, but it does mean that we should pay greater attention to the possibility of a flare-up when we know there is latent conflict that has not been addressed.

THERE ARE NO GREAT TACTICS, ONLY GREAT PRINCIPLES

I am often asked for my opinion on whether a particular strategy or tactic is a good one. These questions are typically expressed along the lines of: *Is it a good idea to _____ in a negotiation?* The problem is that there are very few, if any, strategies or tactics that are universally applicable. There are few such questions that I can answer without knowing more about the situation, without issuing caveats, or without speculating on boundary conditions. The best strategy or tactic is necessarily a function of the analysis one conducts. A strategy that is sound in one case may be disastrous in a slightly different situation. A tactic that failed last time may work next time because the parameters have changed. Not only is it difficult to generalize about the wisdom of a particular tactic; there are also too many tactics to keep track of. There are, ostensibly, an infinite number of negotiation tactics because there are an infinite number of things one could choose to do in a negotiation.

Instead, the key is to focus on the *principles*. The principles are fewer and *are* broadly applicable. These include many of the ideas we have considered throughout the book—for example: control the frame, be mindful of the optics, help the other side save face, have a process strategy, negotiate process before substance, normalize the process, lower the bar for progress, stay at the table, empathize, create slack, work the whole body, map out the negotiation space, seek greater understanding, create value, and so on. What you should do in any one situation will ultimately be a judgment call, but that judgment will be much more sound if you keep these basic principles in mind.

In this way, negotiation is similar to other blends of science and art, such as dance, music, and acting. In the martial arts, for example, students learn many techniques and practice countless combinations tailored for a seemingly infinite number of situations. But the goal is *not* to memorize how one would respond specifically to a particular situation, because there will inevitably be subtle differences between the scenario you studied and the one that confronts you in the moment of attack. Rather, the idea is to understand the science and to practice the techniques in order to learn the principles, because the principles (related to distancing, movement, joint manipulation, balance) will guide you even when you are in a situation you have never encountered before.

The same is true in negotiation; the tactics will vary. I may advise one client to walk away from a deal until the other side softens its demands and another to stay engaged and work towards compromise. I may advise one student to negotiate hard for a better offer from the employer, and another to accept what was offered. I may tell one diplomat or policy maker that he ought to issue an ultimatum and tell another to steer clear of such tactics. I may fight hard for my preferred process in one deal and defer to the other's preferences in the next.

Ideally, you will consider all of the principles before choosing any important course of action. Practically, it is probably better to identify a few of the principles from the book that you think are most relevant to you: things you have not done well or consistently in the past, or ideas that seem most clearly applicable to the problems you face. Once you feel that you are applying these principles consistently and effectively, add more of them to your toolkit.

HUMAN INTERACTION

You need not wait for a tough negotiation to start putting these ideas into practice. We are engaged in countless negotiations every day, and the principles set forth in this book (empathize, ignore or reframe ultimatums, understand the other side's constraints, normalize the process) are as relevant to routine or low-stakes negotiations as they are to the seemingly impossible ones.

In my own negotiating and advising, I find that I am at my best when I remain mindful of the fact that negotiation, regardless of the context or stakes, is about human interaction. When you're dealing with human beings, you should bring the best of what it means to be human. If you can balance assertiveness with empathy, self-confidence with the humility necessary to learn and adapt, and the desire to influence with a genuine interest in understanding, you will be in great shape. The rest is corollaries and details.

This holds regardless of how difficult the situation seems. I tell my children that *every problem wants to be solved.* This is especially true in negotiation. You may not solve it today—it may not even be solvable today—but you will solve it sooner when you remember that all problems of negotiation are, fundamentally, problems of human interaction. Therefore, humans have the capacity to solve them. My hope is that the principles presented in this book will help you to do so even more effectively in the future.

Good luck and best wishes to you on the paths ahead.

NOTES

Introduction: The Most Ancient Lesson in Peacemaking

1. The record for most ancient *arbitration* is held by the deal reached by King Mesilim, which was designed to end the conflict between the city-states of Lagash and Umma, in the Sumer region of Mesopotamia (now Iraq), an agreement that dates back over four thousand years, to 2500 BCE.
2. See Christine Bell, *On the Law of Peace: Peace Agreements and the Lex Pacificatoria* (Oxford: Oxford University Press, 2008), 81.
3. Inevitably, some of the stories involve situations that were even more complex than the versions recounted here: more parties, more forces at play, and more issues at stake. The attempt has been to shine a brighter light on the events and actions that illustrate important and broadly applicable negotiation principles and strategies. Nonetheless, every effort has been made not to over- or underemphasize the role that any one factor played in the ultimate outcomes.
4. Reality is rarely acquiescent to simple classification systems; great stories yield multiple lessons, and skillful negotiators do more than one thing well. Some of the stories could easily fit in more than one section. I have allocated the stories and lessons across the three sections in such a way as to create a narrative that produces a whole that is greater than the sum of its parts.

Chapter 1: The Power of Framing

1. Peter King, "An Unsung Hero in the League Office," *Sports Illustrated*, August 1, 2011.
2. Albeit an oversimplification, if we approximate NFL revenues at $10 billion, the owners' proposal would amount to ~46.4% of all revenues going to players: .58*[10B–2B] = 4.64B.
3. The upper cap in the years 2015–20 would be 48.5%.
4. This is not to say that the two sides were not also trying to out-muscle each other in the media and in the courts.
5. For example, if we have $100 to split between us, and no other issues or interests are at stake, every dollar I get will result in your getting $1 less (and vice versa).

Chapter 2: Leveraging the Power of Framing

1. Some details of this example have been changed or kept out of the story to preserve the anonymity of the people and companies involved. The essence of the story and the relevance of the lessons are unchanged.
2. The table has been modified to ensure that the parties remain anonymous.
3. If you punish your children every time they have the courage to tell you the truth about something they did wrong, don't be surprised if they decide to revise their strategy.

Chapter 3: The Logic of Appropriateness

1. This chapter borrows heavily and takes language directly from the case "Negotiating in the Shadow of Cancer," which was written by Deepak Malhotra (this book's author) and Behfar Ehdaie.
2. PSA screening entails a blood test that measures the levels of the normal enzyme PSA, which is responsible for liquefying semen, to determine if something is wrong in the prostate. An irregularity could be due to infection, cancer, or trauma that disrupts the structure of the prostate and causes more PSA to be released in the blood.
3. Roman Gulati, Lurdes Inoue, John Gore, Jeffrey Katcher, and Ruth Etzioni, "Individualized Estimates of Overdiagnosis in Screen-Detected Prostate Cancer," *Journal of the National Cancer Institute* 106, no. 2 (2014).

4. The appropriateness of active surveillance for a patient depends on many factors that a physician must carefully consider.
5. A more comprehensive description of the intervention is available from the author, Deepak Malhotra.
6. James March and Johan Olsen, "The Logic of Appropriateness," in *The Oxford Handbook of Public Policy*, ed. Robert E. Goodin, Martin Rein, and Michael J. Moran (Oxford: Oxford University Press, 2006).
7. March and Olsen mentioned two other (preliminary) questions that people implicitly consider: *What kind of person am I? What kind of situation is this?* Accordingly, a person will choose differently based on which role or personal identity is salient to him or her at the time (e.g., parent, employee, or citizen), and based on how the situation itself is framed (e.g., is this an ethical or an economic decision?).
8. The research on these topics has been conducted over many decades, by many scholars. For references, and to learn more about these and other related topics, see Deepak Malhotra and Max Bazerman, "Psychological Influence in Negotiation: An Introduction Long Overdue," *Journal of Management* 34, no. 3 (2008): 509–531.
9. Robert Cialdini provides a more comprehensive discussion of this in his book *Influence: The Psychology of Persuasion* (New York: William Morrow & Co., 1993).
10. Behfar Ehdaie, personal communication with the author, 2014.
11. Ibid.
12. The psychological literature more precisely refers to this phenomenon as "anchoring and insufficient adjustment." The idea is that people are aware that the starting point of an analysis (i.e., the *anchor*)—which may be an initial estimate, a first offer from the other side, etc.—might not be the right answer, but merely a point of departure; even so, the starting point is weighted too heavily, and efforts to appropriately adjust away from it tend to be insufficient.
13. Ehdaie, personal communication with the author, 2014.

Chapter 4: Strategic Ambiguity

1. North Korea had signed in 1995, but withdrew in 2003.
2. For more background on these negotiations see, Nicholas Burns, "America's Strategic Opportunity with India: The New U.S.–India Partnership," *Foreign Affairs,* November/December, 2007. And see Jayshree Bajoria and Esther Pan, "The U.S.–India Nuclear Deal," *Council on Foreign Relations,* November 5, 2010.
3. Indeed, both the *Hyde Act* of 2006 that had authorized negotiations with India, as well as the *Atomic Energy Act* (1946 and 1954), would essentially disallow continued nuclear cooperation with India if it detonated a nuclear device.
4. Condoleezza Rice, Congressional Record of the United States Senate, October 1, 2008.
5. "India Will Abide by Unilateral Moratorium on N-tests: Pranab," *The Times of India,* October 3, 2008, http://timesofindia.indiatimes.com/india/India-will-abide-by-unilateral-moratorium-on-N-tests-Pranab/articleshow/3556712.cms. Accessed June 25, 2015.
6. Ibid.

Chapter 5: The Limits of Framing

1. Maggie Farley, "The Big Push for U.N. Council's Support," *Los Angeles Times,* October 12, 2002.
2. See the full text of Resolution 1441 here: http://www.un.org/depts/unmovic/documents/1441.pdf.
3. See the full text of his speech here: http://www.un.org/webcast/usa110802.htm.
4. The term "parasitic" was first introduced in this context by James Gillespie and Max Bazerman in their article "Parasitic integration: Win–win agreements containing losers," *Negotiation Journal* 13, no.3 (1997): 271–282. See also Deepak Malhotra and Max Bazerman, *Negotiation Genius* (New York: Bantam Books, 1997).

Chapter 6: First-Mover Advantage

1. There are over 2,500 National Historic Landmarks. Apart from those located in US states, territories, and commonwealths, the remaining few are in island nations with whom the United States has a "free association" relationship.
2. The treaty was ratified the following year, in 1787, by Congress.
3. Ambassador Tommy Koh made these remarks in 2014 at Harvard University, where he was presented the Great Negotiator Award by the Program on Negotiation, which is based at Harvard Law School. The remarks were made during a panel discussion, as part of the activities surrounding the Great Negotiator event.
4. What follows is from historic accounts kept by the US Department of State, United States Diplomatic Mission to Morocco. See "U.S. Morocco Relations—The Beginning," http://morocco.usembassy.gov/early.html . Accessed June 25, 2015.

Chapter 7: The Power of Process

1. The Articles were not formally ratified by all 13 states until 1781.
2. Some of the details mentioned here are found in Richard Beeman, *Plain, Honest Men: The Making of the American Constitution* (New York: Random House, 2009).
3. Ibid.

Chapter 8: Leveraging the Power of Process

1. Vinod Khosla, personal communication with the author, October 2014.
2. A "financial investor" is someone who invests entirely in hopes of a good future return on the amount invested. A "strategic investor" usually has an interest in the financial outcome of the investment as well, but is someone who sees additional benefits in a relationship with the target company.
3. Two key parameters in any such investment are (a) the amount being invested and (b) the jointly agreed-upon valuation of the company. Taken together, these determine what percentage of ownership is being transferred to the investor. In the case of Sun, the investor would be receiving 10% equity for having invested $10 million in a company perceived as valued at $100 million after the investment.
4. The deal worked out well for all involved. After another 27 years of growing the business, Sun Microsystems was eventually acquired by Oracle in 2010 for over $7 billion.
5. Spoilers are parties whose primary or sole interest in the negotiation is for there to be no deal.
6. Khosla, personal communication, October 2014.

Chapter 9: Preserve Forward Momentum

1. In 1993–94, the two sides tried to negotiate the new CBA under a "no strike, no lockout" pledge on both sides. When this did not yield an agreement, the owners locked out the players at the start of the following season. Since then, a lockout has been initiated each time a CBA has been up for negotiation.
2. The players did not have a labor union for many of those earlier years. The National Hockey League was established in 1917. The Players' Association was formed only in 1967.

Chapter 10: Stay at the Table

1. There were, of course, many other nations present.
2. Eugene White, "The Costs and Consequences of the Napoleonic Reparations," *National Bureau of Economic Research*, working paper no. 7438, December 1999. doi:10.3386/w7438.
3. The Concert of Europe was an offspring of the Quadruple Alliance, whereby Great Britain, Russia, Austria, and Prussia agreed to work together to maintain the European balance of power and enforce the peace that was negotiated in Vienna. France joined this group a few years later, and Great Britain eventually exited.
4. France also accounted for the greatest number of war deaths among the Allies. Only Germany had more deaths among all nations.
5. Margaret MacMillan, *Paris 1919: Six Months That Changed the World* (New York: Random House, 2002), 465.

6. David Fromkin, *A Peace to End All Peace: The Fall of the Ottoman Empire and the Creation of the Modern Middle East* (Macmillan, 1989).
7. Henry Kissinger, *Diplomacy* (New York: Simon & Schuster, 1994).

Chapter 11: The Limits of Process

1. Robert J. Hanyok, "(U) Skunks, Bogies, Silent Hounds, and the Flying Fish: The Gulf of Tonkin Mystery, 2–4 August 1964," *Cryptologic Quarterly* https://www.nsa.gov/public_info/_files/gulf_of_tonkin/articles/rel1_skunks_bogies.pdf. Accessed June 25, 2015.
2. What follows is taken from documents maintained by the US Department of State, Office of the Historian. See "Foreign Relations of the United States, 1964–1968, Volume VII, September 1968–January 1969.," http://history.state.gov/historicaldocuments/frus1964-68v07. Accessed June 25, 2015.
3. Ibid.
4. Ibid.
5. Ibid.

Chapter 12: Changing the Rules of Engagement

1. Ben Blatt, "Which Friends on 'Friends' Were the Closest Friends?" *Slate*, May 4, 2014.
2. Bill Carter, "'Friends' Deal Will Pay Each of Its 6 Stars $22 Million," *New York Times*, February 12, 2002.
3. Robert Hackett, "Jerry Made Serious Cash in the Last Season of 'Seinfeld.'" *Fortune*, June 1, 2015.
4. Brian Lowry, "'Friends' Cast Returning Amid Contract Dispute," *Los Angeles Times*, August 12, 1996.
5. Lynette Rice, "'Friends' Demand a Raise—TV's Top Sitcom Stars Want Another Huge Pay Hike, Meaning the Future of the Show Is Uncertain," *Entertainment Weekly*, April 21, 2000.
6. Warren Littlefield, "With Friends Like These," *Vanity Fair*, May 2012.
7. Carter, "'Friends' Deal Will Pay."
8. Madan M. Pillutla, Deepak Malhotra, and J. Keith Murnighan, "Attributions of trust and the calculus of reciprocity," *Journal of Experimental Social Psychology* 39 (2003): 448–455. doi:10.1016/S0022-1031(03)00015-5.
9. Littlefield, "With Friends Like These."

Chapter 13: The Power of Empathy

1. Simply put, defensive missiles (think "surface to air") could be used to defend against an attack by the United States; offensive missiles (think "surface to surface") could be used to initiate or retaliate against an attack by targeting the United States itself.
2. There are many sources for the further study of the Cuban Missile Crisis. One useful place to start: http://microsites.jfklibrary.org/cmc/.
3. *The Cuban Missile Crisis, 1962: A National Security Archive Documents Reader*, 2nd ed., edited by Laurence Chang and Peter Kornbluh (New York: New Press, 1998), from the foreword by Robert McNamara.
4. Ironically, when President Kennedy ran for president in 1960, he referred to the "missile gap" as being an important issue. He implied, however, that it was the United States that was lagging in nuclear capability, and that he would restore parity. Apparently, neither JFK nor the Soviet Union benefited from acknowledging that the United States was, in fact, far ahead of the Soviet Union.
5. The same might be said of Khrushchev's willingness to understand and respect JFK's constraints.
6. Robert Kennedy, *Thirteen Days: A Memoir of the Cuban Missile Crisis* (New York: W. W. Norton, 1969), 95.
7. Robert McNamara, supplementary interview, *Dr. Strangelove or: How I Learned to Stop Worrying and Love the Bomb* (1964), 40th anniversary release (Columbia Tristar Home Entertainment, 2004) DVD.
8. Kennedy, *Thirteen Days*, 49.
9. Ibid. 43.

Chapter 14: Leveraging the Power of Empathy

1. Some details of this example have been changed to preserve anonymity of the people and companies involved. The essence of the story and the relevance of the lessons are unchanged.

Chapter 15: Yielding

1. Göran Larsson, "'The Invisible Caller': Islamic Opinions on the Use of the Telephone," in *Muslims and the New Media Historical and Contemporary Debates* (Farnham: Ashgate, 2011).
2. "A Chronology: The House of Saud," *Frontline* PBS, http://www.pbs.org/wgbh/pages/frontline/shows/saud/cron/. Accessed June 25, 2015.
3. There is a dark epilogue to this story. Despite King Faisal's success in introducing television to his country, some protests and riots still followed. Among the rioters was one of the king's nephews, Prince Khalid, who was killed during the protests. Almost a decade later, in 1975, Prince Khalid's brother assassinated King Faisal.
4. The trade-off, in a simple sense, is between the reliability and the validity of different performance measures. For example, tenure might be the easiest to measure accurately (high reliability) but be only weakly correlated with performance (low validity). Teacher evaluations, if done well, might be more strongly correlated with performance (high validity) but would be difficult to measure with precision and without bias (low reliability). Student test scores might be somewhere in the middle on reliability and validity.

Chapter 16: Map Out the Negotiation Space

1. The treaty is more commonly known as the *Third Treaty of San Ildefonso*.
2. Carlos Martínez de Yrujo, *To James Madison from Carlos Martínez de Yrujo, 27 September 1803*, National Archives: Founders Online, *Madison Papers*, http://founders.archives.gov/documents/Madison/02-05-02-0470. Accessed June 25, 2015.
3. Robert Livingston, *To James Madison from Robert R. Livingston, 11 July 1803*. National Archives: Founders Online, *Madison Papers*, http://founders.archives.gov/documents/Madison/02-05-02-0204. Accessed June 25, 2015.
4. James Madison, *From James Madison to Robert R. Livingston, 6 October 1803*. National Archives: Founders Online, *Madison Papers*. http://founders.archives.gov/documents/Madison/02-05-02-0504. Accessed June 25, 2015.
5. Robert Livingston and James Monroe, *To James Madison from Robert R. Livingston and James Monroe, 7 June 1803*. National Archives: Founders Online, *Madison Papers*, http://founders.archives.gov/documents/Madison/02-05-02-0085. Accessed June 25, 2015.
6. François Barbé-Marbois, *The History of Louisiana* (Philadelphia: Carey & Lea, 1830), 298–299, http://www.napoleon.org/en/reading_room/articles/files/louisiana_hicks.asp. Accessed June 25, 2015.
7. Thomas Jefferson, *From Thomas Jefferson to Robert R. Livingston, 18 April 1802*, National Archives: Founders Online, *Jefferson Papers*. http://founders.archives.gov/documents/Jefferson/01-37-02-0220. Accessed June 25, 2015.
8. Adolphe Thiers, *Histoire du Consulat*, Livre XVI, March 1803. http://www.napoleon.org/en/reading_room/articles/files/louisiana_hicks.asp. Accessed June 25, 2015.
9. James Monroe, *To James Madison from James Monroe, 14 May 1803*. National Archives: Founders Online, *Madison Papers*, http://founders.archives.gov/documents/Madison/02-04-02-0717. Accessed June 25, 2015.
10. Despite the seemingly low price, many considered the purchased asset to be a distant, useless piece of land. Detractors labeled it "Seward's Folly." It was not until later in the 19th century that gold was discovered on the land. In the 1960s, oil was discovered.
11. Alexander Hamilton, *Purchase of Louisiana, 5 July 1803*. National Archives: Founders Online, http://founders.archives.gov/documents/Hamilton/01-26-02-0001-0101. Accessed June 25, 2015.

12. A little background on how such trades work: Because there are many constraints on teams using money to make trades in the National Basketball Association (NBA), you can't simply write a big check to get the player you want from another team. Instead, you need to structure a trade. A basic trade would involve two teams, each offering up a player that the other wants. If you don't have any players that the other team wants, one option is to include a *future player* in the deal: Team X offers a player it is going to acquire in the future (a "draft pick") in exchange for a player it wants now. A second option is to include *someone else's player* in the deal. Team X wants a player Team Y has, but has nothing of value to give to Team Y. So Team X finds a Team Z that has a player Team Y will want; X makes a trade with Z to get that player, and then uses it to get what it wants from Y. Yet another option is to combine these first two options: get *someone else's future players*. For example, X makes a trade with Z for one of Z's draft picks and includes it in the deal with Y. Things get even more complicated when you add other regulations, such as the team salary cap and luxury tax, which limit how much any team can pay its players in aggregate, in any given year, without incurring hefty penalties.
13. Daryl Morey, personal communication with the author, 2015.
14. Joshua Keating, "The Greatest Doomsday Speeches Never Made," *Foreign Policy*, August 1, 2013.

Chapter 17: Partners, Not Opponents

1. Some details of this example have been changed to preserve anonymity of the people and companies involved. The essence of the story and the relevance of the lessons are unchanged.

Chapter 18: Compare the Maps

1. The people of Kashmir also have their own wide-ranging views on the situation.
2. John Gravois, "The Agnostic Cartographer: How Google's Open-ended Maps Are Embroiling the Company in Some of the World's Touchiest Geopolitical Disputes," *Washington Monthly*, July–August, 2010.
3. The Palestinian Liberation Organization recognized the State of Israel in 1993. The request for recognition "as a Jewish state" is a relatively newer one, perhaps first surfacing in diplomatic engagement around 2007.

Chapter 19: The Path Forward

1. Robert Fish, "Heaven, Hell and Irish Politics," *The Independent*, February 13, 1997.
2. Owen Bowcott, "Northern Ireland's Arch-enemies Declare Peace," *The Guardian*, March 26, 2007.
3. Jonathan Powell, *Talking to Terrorists: How to End Armed Conflicts* (London: Bodley Head, 2014), 217.
4. Ibid., 217.

INDEX

3D Negotiation, 163
123 Agreement, 39–41

A

Adams, Gerry, 194–195
Adams, John, 52
Agreement on Ending the War and Restoring Peace in Vietnam, 103
Alexander II, 164
alternatives, analyzing, 162–163
ambiguity. *See* strategic ambiguity.
analysis-paralysis, 104
Aniston, Jennifer, 111
Anti-Federalists, 66
apologizing for offers, 36–37
appropriateness, logic of, 30–37
AS (active surveillance) for prostate cancer, 28–37
audience, preparing for your argument, 133–134
audience problem, 14

B

backing down from demands, 12–13
Barclay, Thomas, 52, 56–57
barriers to empathy, 142–143
behavior, explaining *vs.* justifying, 128, 141–142
boilerplate, 33–34
books and publications
  3D Negotiation, 163
  "The Agnostic Cartographer," 181
  Agreement on Ending the War and Restoring Peace in Vietnam, 103
  Diplomacy, 95
  Getting Past No, 19
  Great Hatred, Little Room, 185
  Talking to Terrorists, 194–195
  "Vices of the Political System of the United States," 63
Boylan, Arthur, 8
breach of agreement. *See* reneging on an agreement.
breaking deadlocks, 14
bridging, 151–153. *See also* reframing.
Bush, George W., 45

C

Caribbean Crisis. *See* Cuban Missile Crisis.
cartography, role in negotiations, 180–188
case studies
  contract renewal, 53–54
  deadlocks. *See* deadlocks, case studies.
  empathy. *See* empathy, case studies.
  framing. *See* framing, case studies.
  Iraq War, 45–50
  NPT (Non-Proliferation Treaty), 38–44
  in peacemaking. *See* peacemaking, case studies.
  process. *See* process, case studies.
  resistance to change. *See* prostate cancer treatment protocol.
  strategic ambiguity, 38–44
  Sun Microsystems, 68–70, 77
  US–India civil nuclear agreement, 38–44
Castro, Fidel, 124–125
Catholics, in Northern Ireland, 193–195
changing landscapes, 164
Cialdini, Robert, 31
civilian nuclear agreement. *See* NPT (Non-Proliferation Treaty).
clarifying conditions, 154–155
clarity on process
  definition, 72
  failure to achieve, 75
Collins, Michael, 186
commercial agreements
  with a company in China, 135–141
  with an international corporation, 154–155
  royalty rates, 24
commitment to process
  definition, 72
  displaying, 112
  failure to achieve, 75
compliance with appropriate behavior, ensuring, 42–43
concessions, labeling, 113–116
conditions, clarifying, 154–155
confirmation bias, 168–169
conflict, social construction of, 183–184
Congress of Vienna, 90–91
consensus on process, 83–85
constraints, analyzing, 162–163
contract renewal, 53–54
cornering yourself or your opponents, 131–132
cost-benefit analysis, 30–37
credibility
  definition, 130
  safeguarding, 116–117
  vs. strategic flexibility, 130
Cuban Missile Crisis, 122–133, 169, 182
current reality, 186–187
curse of knowledge, 132–133

D

Day of Catastrophe (Naqba), 184–185
deadlocks
- audience problem, 14
- breaking, 14
- creating value, 177
- definition, 5
- over incompatible positions, 13
- partners *vs.* opponents, 176
- preempting *vs.* resolving, 54–56
- zero-sum problem, 14

deadlocks, case studies
- commercial agreements, 24
- NFL negotiations, 8–14, 23–24
- royalty rates, 24

decision making
- apologizing for offers, 36–37
- cost-benefit analysis, 30–37
- justifying offers, 36–37
- leveraging social proof, 31–32
- the logic of appropriateness, 30–37
- promise and perils of uniqueness, 32
- setting the default option, 32–34
- shifting the reference point, 34–36
- value proposition, 37

default option, setting the, 32–34
diffusing the spotlight, 23–24
Diplomacy, 95
DUP (Democratic Unionist Party), 194–195
dynamic assessment, 164

E

Ehdaie, Behfar, 29–37
empathy. *See also* mapping the negotiation space; partners *vs.* opponents.
- avoid cornering yourself or your opponents, 131–132
- barriers to, 142–143
- the beginning of history, 185–186
- bridging, 151–153
- characteristics of great negotiators, 134
- clarifying conditions, 154–155
- confirmation bias, 168–169
- creating options, 126–127
- creating slack in triggers for retaliation, 129–130
- current reality, 186–187
- curse of knowledge, 132–133
- explaining behavior *vs.* justifying it, 128, 141–142
- forgetting the past, 186–187
- premature strategy selection, 168–169
- preparing your argument *vs.* preparing your audience, 133–134
- psychological barriers, 142
- social construction of conflict, 183–184
- strategic flexibility *vs.* credibility, 130
- structural barriers, 142
- tactical barriers, 143
- for those who least deserve it, 128
- timing of negotiations, 147–148
- ultimatums, 131, 144–146
- understanding the sacred, 184–185
- working the whole body, 143–144
- yielding, 150–151, 153–155

empathy, case studies
- cartography and linguistics, 180–188
- commercial agreement with company in China, 135–141
- Cuban Missile Crisis, 122–133, 169
- Houston Rockets draft pick, 167–168
- an international corporation, 154–155
- Israel/Palestine agreement, 184–185
- a JDA (Joint Development Agreement), 135–141
- Louisiana Purchase, 156–166
- map of India, 180–188
- modernity in Saudi Arabia, 149–150
- partners *vs.* opponents, 171–175
- teacher salaries, 152–153
- value-maximizing outcomes, 171–175

ensuring the opponent's safety, 19–20
examples. *See* case studies.

F

Faisal, King, 149–150, 153
FARC (Revolutionary Armed Forces of Colombia), 82–83
Federalists, 66
final agreement, 86
first-mover advantage
- in framing, 52–53
- setting defaults, 33

flexibility
- process, 78–79
- structure, 26
- style, 26

forgetting the past, 186–187
forward momentum, preserving, 82–83
framing. *See also* reframing.
- apologizing for offers, 36–37
- building trust, 19–20
- challenging a disadvantageous frame, 115–116
- cost-benefit analysis, 30–37
- decision making, 30–37
- definition, 11
- diffusing the spotlight, 23–24
- ensuring the opponent's safety, 19–20
- flexibility on style and structure, 26
- getting unstuck as a short-term goal, 26
- high-leverage moments, 56–57
- holding firm on substance, 26
- incompatible positions, 25
- justifying offers, 36–37
- leveraging social proof, 31–32
- limits of, 45–50
- the logic of appropriateness, 30–37
- negotiating issues simultaneously, 22–23
- one-issue negotiations, 21–22
- optics of the deal, 18–19
- package offers, 22–23
- positions *vs.* interests, 25
- promise and perils of uniqueness, 32
- relationships based on equality, 57
- resistance to change. *See* prostate cancer treatment protocol.
- selling the deal, 19–20
- setting the default option, 32–34
- shifting the reference point, 34–36
- splitting issues, 24
- strategic ambiguity, 38–44
- unmasking underlying interests, 25
- value proposition, 37
- writing the opponent's victory speech, 19–20

framing, case studies
- commercial agreements, 15–18
- Iraq War, 45–50
- NFL negotiations, 8–14, 23–24
- prostate cancer treatment protocol, 28–37
- royalty agreement, 15–18

France, and the Napoleonic Wars, 89–91, 93–94
Friends TV show, 109–117

G

George, Lloyd, 186
Germany, after WW I, 89–91, 93–94
Getting Past No, 19
getting unstuck as a short-term goal, 26
good fortune, preparing for, 165–166
Good Friday Agreement, 193–195
Google map sites, 181
Great Hatred, Little Room, 185
Great Negotiator Award, 134
Gulf of Tonkin incidents, 98
Gulf of Tonkin Resolution, 98

H

Hamilton, Alexander, 165
Harden, James, 167–168
Hattusili III, 1
high-leverage moments in framing, 56–57
history, beginning of, 185–186
Houston Rockets draft pick, 167–168
human interaction, role in negotiation, 5, 197–198
Hussein, Saddam, 45
Hyde Act (2006), 39

I

Ibn Saud, 149–150
ICAP (Interests, Constraints, Alternatives, Perspective) analysis, 162–163
implementing the results of process, 65–66
incompatible positions, 25
Independence Day (Yom Ha'atzmaut), 184–185
India–US civil nuclear agreement, 38–44
insufficient groundwork for process, 104
interests
- analyzing, 162–163
- underlying, unmasking, 25
- *vs.* positions, 25

international corporation, commercial agreement with, 154–155
IRA (Irish Republican Army), 193–195
Iraq War, 45–50
Israel/Palestine agreement, 184–185

J

JDA (Joint Development Agreement), 135–141
Jefferson, Thomas, 52, 158–159, 165
JFK. *See* Kennedy, John F..
Johnson, Lyndon, 98–103
justifying offers, 36–37

K

keeping your word, 116–117
Kennedy, John F., 122–133, 169, 182, 188
Kennedy, Robert, 122–123, 128, 131–132
Khosla, Vinod, 68–70, 78
Khrushchev, Nikita, 123–127, 131, 182
Kissinger, Henry, 95
Koh, Tommy, 54–56

L

labeling concessions, 113–116
Lax, David, 163
LeBlanc, Matt, 114–115
legitimacy, process as proxy war for, 105–106
leverage, process as proxy war for, 105–106
leveraging social proof, 31–32
linguistics, role in negotiations, 180–188
Livingston, Robert, 156–158
lockouts
- definition, 80
- in the NHL, 80–81, 147–148

logic of appropriateness, 30–37
Louisiana Purchase, 156–166
low bar for progress, high bar for agreement, 85

M

Madison, James
- Louisiana Purchase, 157–159
- negotiating the US Constitution, 61–64, 155

mapping the negotiation space
- action away from the table, 163–165
- alternatives, analyzing, 162–163
- changing landscapes, 164
- constraints, analyzing, 162–163
- creating option value, 166–168
- description, 161
- dynamic assessment, 164
- ICAP analysis, 162–163
- improving positioning, 166–168
- interests, analyzing, 162–163
- Louisiana Purchase, 156–165
- perspective, analyzing, 162–163
- preparing for good fortune, 165–166
- relevant parties, 161
- role of third parties, 163–165
- static assessment, 164
- strategic assessment, 164
- trilateral thinking, 160–161

maps
- Google map sites, 181
- role in negotiations, 180–188

McGuinness, Martin, 185, 194–195
McNamara, Robert, 124
McNealy, Scott, 68–70
mediator's tactic, 73
Mohammed III, 52
Monroe, James, 159
Morey, Daryl, 167–168
Moroccan-American Treaty of Friendship, 51–52
MSKCC (Memorial Sloan Kettering Cancer Center), 28
Mukherjee, Pranab, 41, 42

N

Napoleon, 156–164
Napoleonic Wars, 89–91, 93–94
Naqba (Day of Catastrophe), 184–185
Nationalists, 193–195
negotiation
- crucial levers. *See* empathy; framing; process.
- definition, 4–5
- in human interaction, 197–198
- one-issue, 21–22
- on simultaneous issues, 22–23
- tactics *vs.* principles, 196–197
- timing of, 147–148

negotiation space, mapping. *See* mapping the negotiation space.
negotiators, characteristics of, 134
Negroponte, John, 46
NFL negotiations, 8–14, 23–24, 177
NHL strikes and lockouts, 80–81, 147–148, 177
NLF (National Liberation Front), 98
normalizing process, 72–75
Northern Ireland conflict, 185–186, 193–195
NPT (Non-Proliferation Treaty), 38–44
NSG (Nuclear Suppliers Group), 39
nuclear agreement between the US and India. *See* NPT (Non-Proliferation Treaty).

O

October Crisis. *See* Cuban Missile Crisis.
one-issue negotiations, 21–22
123 Agreement, 39–41
opponents *vs.* partners. *See* partners *vs.* opponents.
optics of the deal, 18–19
option value, creating, 166–168
order-of-speaking negotiations, 100–103

P

package offers, 22–23
Paisley, Ian, 194–195
Palestine/Israel agreement, 184–185
parasitic agreement, 48–50
parasitic value creation, 49
Paris Peace Accords, 103
partners *vs.* opponents
  case study, 171–175
  creating value, 176
  deadlocks, 176
  imagining the impossible, 178–179
  ugly conflicts, 176
  value-maximizing solutions, 177
peacemaking, case studies
  Congress of Vienna, 90–91
  France, and the Napoleonic Wars, 89–91, 93–94
  Germany, after WW I, 89–91, 93–94
  Napoleonic Wars, 89–91, 93–94
  Paris Peace Accords, 103
  between warring factions, 55–56
  WW I, 89–91, 93–94
peacemaking, underinvestment in process during time of peace, 95–97
perspective, analyzing, 162–163
Pierce, William, 67
positioning, improving, 166–168
positions *vs.* interests, 25
Powell, Johnathan, 185, 194–195
preempting deadlocks *vs.* resolving, 54–56
preserving forward momentum, 82–83
principles, *vs.* tactics, 196–197
process
  achieving full agreement, 78–79
  addressing substantive concerns, 108
  analysis-paralysis, 104
  bypassing, 104–105
  challenging destructive patterns, 115–116
  clarity and commitment, 72, 75
  consensus, 83–85
  definition, 64
  desire for strategic flexibility, 104
  elements of, 64–65
  final agreement, 86
  flexibility, 78–79
  implementation, 65–66
  insufficient groundwork, 104
  keeping your word, 116–117
  labeling concessions, 113–116
  low bar for progress, high bar for agreement, 85
  mediator's tactic, 73
  negotiating before substance, 70–71
  negotiating in parallel with substance, 108
  normalizing, 72–75
  order-of-speaking negotiations, 100–103
  preparing for, 67
  preserving forward momentum, 82–83
  proxy wars for leverage and legitimacy, 105–106
  reasons for getting stuck, 103–104
  resolving residual conflict, 91–92
  rules of engagement, 109–117
  safeguarding credibility, 116–117
  seeking equality and not advantage, 108
  shaping, 63–65
  showing commitment to, 112
  staying at the table, 92–94
  sufficient consensus, 84–85
  synchronizing with other parties, 71
  table-shape negotiations, 99–103, 105–106
  taking a stand on, 106–108
  transparency in the bargaining process, 86–88
  underinvestment during time of peace, 95–97
  vs. substance, 104–106
  without a seat at the table, 94
process, case studies
  Friends TV show, 109–117
  negotiating a strategic partnership, 106–107
  negotiating the US Constitution, 60–63
  NHL strikes and lockouts, 80–81, 147–148
  reneging on an agreement, 68–70, 77
  Vietnam War, 98–103
prostate cancer treatment protocol, 28–37
Protestants, in Northern Ireland, 193–195
proxy wars for leverage and legitimacy, 105–106
PSA (prostate-specific antigen), 28
psychological barriers to empathy, 142
psychological lens, 11

R

Ramesses II, 1
Randolph, Edmund, 63
reference point, shifting the, 34–36
reframing. *See also* framing.
  bridging, 151–153
  as early as possible, 53–54
  ultimatums, 146
  yielding, 150–151
relationships based on equality, 57
relevant parties, 161
reneging on an agreement
  case study, 68–70, 77
  managing risk of, 76
  walking away from, 76–78
residual conflict, resolving, 91–92
resistance to change. *See* prostate cancer treatment protocol.
Resolution 1441, 46
resolving deadlocks *vs.* preempting, 54–56
resolving residual conflict, 91–92
Revolutionary Armed Forces of Colombia (FARC), 82–83
Rice, Condoleezza, 40–41
royalty rates, 15–18, 24
rules of engagement, 109–117

S

the sacred, understanding, 184–185
safeguarding credibility, 116–117
safety, ensuring for the opponent, 19–20
Saudi Arabia, selling modernity, 149–150
Schwimmer, David, 109–116
Sebenius, James, 163
Shay's Rebellion, 60–61
Sinn Fein, 185–186, 193–195
slack in triggers for retaliation, creating, 129–130
social construction of conflict, 183–184
social proof, leveraging, 31–32
splitting issues, 24
static assessment, 164
staying at the table, 92–94
strategic ambiguity
  case studies. *See* Iraq War; NPT (Non-Proliferation Treaty).
  compliance with appropriate behavior, 42–43
  description, 41–42
  in early relationships, 42–43
  parasitic agreement, 48–50
  parasitic value creation, 49
  as substitute for agreement, 47
  tradeoff between current and future conflicts, 47–48
  when there is no substantive agreement, 48

strategic assessment, 164
strategic flexibility, 130
strategic partnership, negotiating, 106–107
strategy, selecting prematurely, 168–169
strikes
  definition, 80
  in the NHL, 80–81, 147–148
structural barriers to empathy, 142
structure, flexibility, 26
style, flexibility, 26
substance
  holding firm on, 26
  negotiating in parallel with process, 108
  vs. process, 104–106
sufficient consensus, 84–85

T

table-shape negotiations, 99–103, 105–106
tactical barriers to empathy, 143
tactics *vs.* principles, 196–197
Tallyrand, 93
teacher salaries, 152–153
third parties, in mapping negotiation space, 163–165
Third UN Conference of the Law of the Sea (1973–1982), 54
3D Negotiation, 163
transparency in the bargaining process, 86–88
treaties
  Moroccan-American Treaty of Friendship, 51–52
  NPT (Non-Proliferation Treaty), 38–44
  oldest in US history, 51–52
  Treaty of Kadesh, 1–2
  Treaty on the Non-Proliferation of Nuclear Weapons, 38–44
Treaty of Kadesh, 1–2
Treaty on the Non-Proliferation of Nuclear Weapons, 38–44
trilateral thinking, 160–161
trust, building, framing, 19–20

U

U-2 spy plane, 129–130
ugly conflicts
  creating value, 177
  definition, 5–6
  partners *vs.* opponents, 176
ultimatums, 131, 144–146
UN Security Council Resolution 1441, 46
underinvestment in process during time of peace, 95–97
understanding the sacred, 184–185
Unionists, 193–195
uniqueness, promise and perils of, 32
unmasking underlying interests, 25
Ury, William, 19
US Constitution, negotiating, 60–63
US–India civil nuclear agreement, 38–44

V

value, creating in deadlocks, 177
value proposition, 37
"Vices of the Political System of the United States," 63
Vickers, Andrew, 29
victory speech, helping the opponent write, 19–20
Viet Cong, 98
Vietnam War, 98–103
Virginia Plan, 62–63

W

walking away from process conflict, 76–78
War Guilt Clause, 90–91
Washington, George, 60, 62–63
Wavell, Earl, 93
working the whole body, 143–144
writing the opponent's victory speech, 19–20
WW I, 89–91, 93–94

Y

yielding, 150–151, 153–155. *See also* reframing.
Yom Ha'atzmaut (Independence Day), 184–185

Z

zero-sum problem, 14, 21–22

ACKNOWLEDGMENTS

IT HAS BEEN ALMOST 20 years since I first walked into his office as a grad student at the Kellogg School of Management, but Keith Murnighan continues to play the role of advisor and mentor. When I asked him to comment on an earlier draft of this book, he went through it like it was 1998. It came back to me with over 1,500 minor edits—in a manuscript that has less than 70,000 words! Keith is a force of nature—tireless, wise, kind, and generous—and I am lucky to have him as a friend.

Harvard Business School, my academic home for almost 15 years, could not be a more supportive and inspiring place to work. My colleagues in the Negotiation, Organizations, and Markets Unit are like family. My thanks to Max Bazerman, John Beshears, Alison Wood Brooks, Amy Cuddy, Ben Edelman, Christine Exley, Francesca Gino, Jerry Green, Brian Hall, Leslie John, Mike Luca, Kathleen McGinn, Kevin Mohan, Matt Rabin, Jim Sebenius, Joshua Schwartzstein, Guhan Subramanian, Andy Wasynczuk, and Mike Wheeler. Max Bazerman, my co-author on *Negotiation Genius*, deserves an additional thank-you for introducing me to book writing, and for his continued guidance in all aspects of academic life. Also at HBS, I owe special thanks to Dean Nitin Nohria for always being an enthusiastic supporter of my (occasionally unorthodox) academic endeavors.

Cody Smith and Elizabeth Sweeny provided many helpful comments on the manuscript. I inflicted more drafts of the book on Cody than on anyone else, but he was nice enough to tell me that he never got bored with it. (I have my doubts.) I am also thankful to Wally Bock, Thomas Kruse, and David Marshall for their very helpful feedback on the first full draft.

The book would not be in your hands without the hard work of the excellent folks at Berrett-Koehler. If you ever want to publish a book, look them up. Special thanks to Steve Piersanti for his feedback and guidance through every phase of the process. Steve's enthusiasm for me and my work has always been more than I deserve, and I am grateful.

Thanks to Jonathan Powell, a colleague and friend. When it comes to navigating the world of armed conflicts, there could be no better guide or companion than he. It has been a pleasure learning from you, and working with you to make a difference where it matters most.

I am also indebted to the many thousands of students, executives, and business owners I have had the privilege of teaching, and to the hundreds of businesses I have had the pleasure of training and advising. Your most difficult questions about seemingly impossible problems motivated me to develop the ideas in this book, and your enthusiasm for the ideas I shared with you inspired me to write them down.

Most of all, I am grateful for my family. My parents, Chander and Sudesh Malhotra, and my brother, Manu Malhotra, have been a source of strength and optimism from my earliest memories. My parents were the first to provide feedback on this book when it was just a collection of stories; they were also the last people to provide edits on the final draft. My wife, Shikha, not only provides feedback and encouragement for all of my endeavors, but also is singlehandedly responsible for creating a world in which I am able to pursue my work and take on a project like this. Your hard work and sacrifices overwhelm the capacity of words to convey the level of appreciation you deserve. Finally, my children—Jai, Aria, and Aisha—are a constant reminder that it is worth trying to make the world a better, safer, and more enjoyable place for everyone . . . and that doing so is possible.